THE SOMEWHAT TRUE TALE OF ROBIN HOOD

by
MARY LYNN DOBSON

Dramatic Publishing
Woodstock, Illinois • England • Australia • New Zealand

*** NOTICE ***

The amateur and stock acting rights to this work are controlled exclusively by THE DRAMATIC PUBLISHING COMPANY without whose permission in writing no performance of it may be given. Royalty must be paid every time a play is performed whether or not it is presented for profit and whether or not admission is charged. A play is performed any time it is acted before an audience. Current royalty rates, applications and restrictions may be found at our website: www.dramaticpublishing.com, or we may be contacted by mail at: DRAMATIC PUBLISHING COMPANY, 311 Washington St., Woodstock IL 60098.

COPYRIGHT LAW GIVES THE AUTHOR OR THE AUTHOR'S AGENT THE EXCLUSIVE RIGHT TO MAKE COPIES. This law provides authors with a fair return for their creative efforts. Authors earn their living from the royalties they receive from book sales and from the performance of their work. Conscientious observance of copyright law is not only ethical, it encourages authors to continue their creative work. This work is fully protected by copyright. No alterations, deletions or substitutions may be made in the work without the prior written consent of the publisher. No part of this work may be reproduced or transmitted in any form or by any means, electronic or mechanical, including photocopy, recording, videotape, film, or any information storage and retrieval system, without permission in writing from the publisher. It may not be performed either by professionals or amateurs without payment of royalty. All rights, including, but not limited to, the professional, motion picture, radio, television, videotape, foreign language, tabloid, recitation, lecturing, publication and reading, are reserved.

For performance of any songs, music and recordings mentioned in this play which are in copyright, the permission of the copyright owners must be obtained or other songs and recordings in the public domain substituted.

©MM by
MARY LYNN DOBSON
Printed in the United States of America
All Rights Reserved
(THE SOMEWHAT TRUE TALE OF ROBIN HOOD)

For inquiries concerning all other rights, contact:
Stanley F. Werse Esq., Katich, Werse & Petillo,
823 River Rd., Fair Haven NJ 07704

ISBN: 1-58342-013-4

IMPORTANT BILLING AND CREDIT REQUIREMENTS

All producers of the play *must* give credit to the author of the play in all programs distributed in connection with performances of the play and in all instances in which the title of the play appears for purposes of advertising, publicizing or otherwise exploiting the play and/or a production. The name of the author *must* also appear on a separate line, on which no other name appears, immediately following the title, and *must* appear in size of type not less than fifty percent (50%) the size of the title type. Biographical information on the author, if included in the playbook, may be used in all programs. *In all programs this notice must appear:*

"Produced by special arrangement with
THE DRAMATIC PUBLISHING COMPANY of Woodstock, Illinois"

WHAT PEOPLE ARE SAYING about *The Somewhat True Tale of Robin Hood.*

"Excellent! It is funny and witty. My 7th- & 8th-graders enjoyed working on it and seeing it. I hope to be able to direct this one again. I would love to act in it. We added physical, visual humor to the great dialogue." *Doug Dixon,*
Carman-Ainsworth Junior High, Flint, Mich.

"This is a very clever play, good for many ages. For instance, opening night I sat between a 5-year-old and a 20-something—both enjoyed it immensely. My wife (40), not often charmed by children's plays, had a great time as well." *Bruce Tinker,*
Grand Rapids Civic Theatre, Grand Rapids, Mich.

"Everyone enjoyed it very much—old folks down to primary grades. It was funny, in good taste and fun to perform—enough action to suit the teen boys and enough female parts to look pretty." *Lucy Hannegan,*
St. Louis Catholic Home Association, St. Louis, Mo.

"*Robin Hood* is perfect for middle-schoolers. It gives so many kids a chance to be part of a production without too much pressure. At the same time it presents a challenge for the leads. Jokes that stand on their own help immensely." *Kevin Appleby,*
Bunker Hill Middle School, Sewell, N.J.

The Somewhat True Tale of Robin Hood is a wonderfully funny, well-written spoof on the traditional tale. Bumbling merry men complete w/ wooden spoons for swords, a skin-condition-obsessed Lady Marian and an egotistical Robin make for a great script. *Mary Jane Smith,*
Hamden Hall Country Day School, Hamden, Conn.

To my darling Jim

pebble…pebble…

THE SOMEWHAT TRUE TALE OF ROBIN HOOD opened at Playhouse 22, East Brunswick, N.J., on July 16, 1999. The production was directed by Mary Lynn Dobson and included the following artists:

CAST

Robin Hood	THOMAS A. THORPE
Lady Marian	FAITH AGNEW
Town's Guy	SETH BISEN-HERSH
Prince John	CHRIS LOWRY
Sheriff of Nottingham	JEFF DWORKIN
Friar Tuck	CHARLES N. GIRARD
Will Scarlet	JODY BARDIN
Allan Adale	PATRICK GIANOTTO
Little John	RICHARD LEN MCCARTY
Lady In Waiting	ROSSLYN D. DAVIS
The Fawning Ladies	STACY ALBENICE
	CARRIE SUZANNE COUZENS
	KIRSTEN LIEDAHL
	KATHLEEN LOCKARD

PRODUCTION STAFF

Producer	PETER RIGA JR.
Associate Producer	AMY LEVINE
Set Design	JIM PARKS SR. and VAUNE PECK
Lighting	PATRICK GIANOTTO
Costumes	JAMES HERRERA
Production Stage Manager	BARBARA GIANOTTO

THE SOMEWHAT TRUE TALE OF ROBIN HOOD

A Play in Two Acts
For 8 men and 6 women*

CHARACTERS

ROBIN HOOD . . . . Dashing hero with a large ego.
LADY MARIAN . . . . Lovely damsel in distress.
PRINCE JOHN . . . . The head bad guy.
SHERIFF OF NOTTINGHAM . . Prince John's cohort in crime.
TOWN'S GUY . . . . The local-yokel.
LADY IN WAITING . . . . Lady Marian's attendant.
FRIAR TUCK. . . . . Holy relic.
WILL SCARLET . . . . The wise guy.
LITTLE JOHN . . . . Big lummox with an I. Q. of six.
ALLAN ADALE . . . . Slightly brighter than Little John.
FAWNING LADIES . . Four ladies who "fawn" over Prince John.
GUARDS (2) . . . . Can be cast singly or doubled by male Merry Men wearing long black robes and black hooded masks.
RICH MAN . . Can be cast singly or doubled by the actor playing Prince John. (Non-speaking role.)
POOR LADY WITH A BABY . . Can be cast singly or doubled by a Fawning Lady. (Non-speaking role.)

*The cast as described here is the most popular casting for this show. However, if you require a larger cast, please see the supplemented scene in the production notes at the end of the script. With the addition of this scene, the cast can be expanded to 25 or more with new roles for either male or female actors. Should your production require a smaller cast, there are also directions on how to condense the cast size to 10.

Additional character notes can be found at end of playbook.

ACT ONE

(Happy, lighthearted folk music can be played before curtain. The curtain should rise as the music is ending.)

SCENE: *Sherwood Forest. We are among the trees and the greenery, as typical forest sounds are heard, such as birds chirping, etc.*

AT RISE: *Lights come up on TOWN'S GUY, who is standing by a tree.*

TOWN'S GUY. Good day to you all, good folk! Welcome to Sherwood Forest. This is a place of lore and legends. A place which the most famous characters of all time came to call home. Characters of strength. Characters of virtue. Characters such as...Robin Hood and his Merry Men.

(Gestures to ROBIN and the MEN. ROBIN HOOD stands center. LITTLE JOHN is on his hands and knees, looking at the ground. His head should face the audience. A MERRY MAN is on either side of LITTLE JOHN. They use him as a table and are playing cards. The FRIAR stands, watching. Note: The MEN do not have their spoons with them in this scene. The MEN are engrossed in their game as ROBIN laments.)

ROBIN. Oh Merry Men, Merry Men! My heart is full of grief! It weighs heavy upon my soul. You gaze on one whose brightest light has been snuffed by the dark blanket of gloom. There is nothing left for me but sorrow and despair! *(To WILL.)* Play the jack. *(Back to lamenting.)* Stands before you a man who suffers from the anguish of unrequited love! There are no means to describe my agony, Merry Men, except to say…I have the boo-boos.

MEN *(to AUDIENCE, in unison, they gasp)*. OH NO! NOT THE BOO-BOOS! *(They resume playing cards.)*

ROBIN. Yes, I know you're shocked! I realize great characters of literature rarely get the boo-boos, but, I have them today. My one and only love, Lady Marian, is lost to me forever! How can I go on?

LITTLE *(to ALLAN as he places a pewter mug on the "table"—his back)*. Hey, hey, hey! Use your coaster! *(ALLAN obliges.)*

ROBIN. Soon the woman of my dreams will wed that incomparable bad guy, the Sheriff of Nottingham. And from that very moment on, Merry Men… *(Front.)* LIFE WILL HAVE NO MEANING! Once she marries him, he and the Prince will conspire to control all the land. Oh, what to do! What to do!

TOWN'S GUY. Well, first you could explain to the good folk who the Sheriff and the Prince are.

ROBIN *(stares at him a moment)*. Well yes, I suppose I could. *(To AUDIENCE.)* Gentle folk, our beloved England was once ruled by a great sovereign, King Richard the Lion Hearted.

MEN *(to AUDIENCE, in unison)*. LONG LIVE THE KING!

Act I ROBIN HOOD 11

ROBIN. Our courageous king left us to fight in the crusades. In his absence, we have been ruled by his rotten, sinister and not at all nice brother, THE EVIL PRINCE JOHN.
MEN *(to AUDIENCE, quickly in unison)*. BOO, HISS! BOO, HISS!
ROBIN. You see, Prince John wants to be crowned king. Since King Richard has been gone for more than two years, law decrees that Prince John may take the crown *if* he is elected by another member of the royal family.
TUCK. But, Robin, the only other royal is the fair Lady Marian. She loathes the Prince severely and would never dream of letting him become king. *(To AUDIENCE.)* She wishes him only skin rashes.
MEN. Eew!
ROBIN. True, Friar, but acting as ruler, law decrees that THE EVIL PRINCE JOHN…
MEN *(to AUDIENCE, quickly in unison)*. BOO, HISS! BOO, HISS!
ROBIN. …may give dear Marian's hand in marriage to a suitor of his choice. His choice is the Sheriff of Nottingham. And as we all know, the Sheriff of Nottingham is…well, he's…he's a worm! The man's a worm! A slimy, slithering little worm. You just want to squash him flat with your foot and then scrape him off your shoe. Anyway, once the Sheriff marries Marian, he will instantly become royalty. Thus giving the Sheriff the power to allow Prince John to be king! And what a grim day for all it will be! The Prince's greed knows no limits. Why, the Prince isn't even king yet and already he's raised taxes sky high!
MEN *(to AUDIENCE, in unison)*. NO!

ROBIN. Closed schools and orphanages!

MEN *(to AUDIENCE, in unison)*. NO!

ROBIN. And most despicable of all... *(Dramatic pause.)* ...he's stopped the sale of Girl Scout cookies.

MEN *(to AUDIENCE, in unison)*. OH NO! NOT THAT!

TUCK. Even Chocolate Thin Mints, my son?

ROBIN. Yes, Friar, even those.

TUCK. Merciful heaven, help us!

TOWN'S GUY. I'll say! I mean, I can see banishing the Lemon Cremes because, well hey, let's face it, who buys them anyway? But no more Thin Mints! Why, I would indeed rebel against that!

ROBIN *(stares at him a moment)*. Excuse me, but...who are you?

TOWN'S GUY. Me? I'm the Town's Guy.

ROBIN *(stares at him a moment)*. I see. And what exactly is it that you do?

TOWN'S GUY. Well, I...hang around the town, hence the name, Town's Guy. This isn't rocket science here. *(Gives ROBIN a friendly little punch in the arm.)*

ROBIN. Oh. How productive. Then may I ask, what are you doing here? If you haven't noticed, this is the forest.

TOWN'S GUY. Well, yes, I know. I just thought I'd hang around here and help you tell the story.

ROBIN. That's quite nice, but to be honest with you, we don't need your help. Please leave.

TOWN'S GUY *(insulted)*. Well, fine! I was going to set up the scene when you first met Lady Marian, but hey, you don't need me! Introduce your own flashback!

MEN *(to AUDIENCE, in unison)*. FLASHBACK?!

TUCK. Oh, Robin, please. You know how much the Merry Men do love a good flashback.

Act I ROBIN HOOD 13

MEN *(to ROBIN, chanting in unison)*. FLASHBACK! FLASHBACK! FLASHBACK!

ROBIN *(to MERRY MEN)*. You know, that's really getting on my nerves. *(To TOWN'S GUY.)* Oh, very well. If you must do a flashback get on with it.

TOWN'S GUY. All right, I'll do it. But as soon as this flashback flashbacks forward again…I'm outta here. *(Calls out to the technical director.)* Mr. Technical Director, good day to you, sir. *(Waves to him.)* Some flashback atmosphere, if you please.*

MEN *(lights dim as they exit)*. FLASHBACK! FLASHBACK! FLASHBACK!

ROBIN *(in the dark)*. STOP THAT!

TOWN'S GUY. You see, good folk, Robin Hood robbed from the rich and gave to the poor. *(During this we see ROBIN robbing a MAN of his bag of money. The MAN runs off L.)* Now, we all know it's wrong to steal. But it was Prince John who had stolen the good people of England's money first! The money Robin Hood and his men would take from the rich countrymen would buy food and clothes for starving families. *(ROBIN gives the money to a WOMAN carrying a BABY. He hands her the pouch, gives the BABY a "coochie-coo" under the chin.)* That was the only way the poor people could survive. *(The WOMAN thanks him with a curtsy and exits R. ROBIN exits L.)* And even though I think Robin is one outlaw with an attitude problem, he is the champion of those less fortunate. On this day I take you to now,

---

* To suit the gender of the technical director, this may be changed to "Miss," "Ms." or "Mrs." Technical Director. You may make the appropriate adjustment throughout the rest of the play as well.

Robin came upon one of the richest and most powerful men in the country.

(Lights up. SHERIFF enters with LADY MARIAN. He is carrying a large pouch of money and she is carrying a small chest of jewels.)

SHERIFF. I can't believe our carriage is stuck in the mud. I am sorry to make you carry that chest, Marian, my dear, but with the recent series of robberies, I thought it best not to leave it where it may encounter unwanted hands. But, fear not! I shall find the way out of this dark and creepy forest.
MARIAN. I think it's quite a warm and friendly place.

(ROBIN enters.)

ROBIN. Halt! Surrender your money to me, please!
SHERIFF. I do say, we're being mugged. How warm and friendly.
MARIAN. Well, at least he said please. I do think manners count for something.
ROBIN. Thank you, my lady.
SHERIFF. Marian, I believe we are in the company of the notorious outlaw, Robin Hood.
ROBIN. In the flesh.
SHERIFF. And you alone plan on ridding me of my riches?

(MEN enter running, screaming at the top of their lungs.)

MEN. AHHHHH! *(Note: The spoons should not be seen until this moment. In unison, they draw their spoons as if*

Act I ROBIN HOOD 15

they were drawing their swords. When the "swords" are revealed, we see that they are actually large mixing spoons. They point their spoons at the SHERIFF.) AH HA!

ROBIN. You seem to be outnumbered, sir.

MARIAN. Why, Sheriff, this must be Robin Hood's band of married men.

ROBIN. That's Merry Men, my lady. *(MERRY MEN quickly and in unison, smile and wave to MARIAN, then return to pointing their spoons at the SHERIFF.)* Let me assure, charming lady, we are all quite single gentlemen.

LITTLE *(scratching under his arm with his spoon).* Why, I don't even got meself a girlfriend. *(Wipes his nose on his sleeve.)*

MARIAN *(matter-of-factly).* And what a shock that is.

ROBIN. Now, if you don't mind, dear guests, your treasures, please.

TOWN'S GUY. And with that, Robin snatched the bag of gold from the Sheriff.

ROBIN. AH HA! *(Grabs the bag.)*

TOWN'S GUY. And then he grabbed Marian's chest.[*] *(All stop dead and look at the TOWN'S GUY.)* THE ONE SHE IS HOLDING IN HER HANDS THAT CONTAINS THE JEWELS.

MEN. Oh! *(MARIAN smiles nervously and hands ROBIN the chest of jewels.)*

ROBIN *(uneasy).* Ah… Thank you.

---

[*] The chest joke is only a play on words. Neither Robin nor the Merry Men should glare at Marian's chest. Marian should not heave her chest, etc. This is for young audiences, so there should be no other references to Marian's physical chest whatsoever. Should the line be questionable to be performed by a school or a young cast, it may be changed to: "And then he grabbed the chest of jewels from Marian." Then, cut to Sheriff's line, "You won't get away with this, you scoundrel!"

MARIAN. Of course. *(Out of the corner of her mouth to the SHERIFF.)* Next time, I carry the pouch.

SHERIFF. You won't get away with this, you scoundrel! This gold belongs to none other than His Royal Highness!

ROBIN. Are you speaking of...THE EVIL PRINCE JOHN?

MEN *(to AUDIENCE, quickly in unison)*. BOO, HISS! BOO, HISS!

SHERIFF. That's your opinion. Yes, it is his gold you rob!

ROBIN. Then, it is with all the more pleasure that I lighten your load of this tarnished gold.

MARIAN. Hasn't anyone ever taught you that stealing is wrong?

ROBIN. I don't consider this stealing, dear lady. I am merely returning it to those from whom it was taken. Because of sheer greed from ones like the Prince and Sheriff, people, young and old, are starving. Children cry at night, frightened, cold and hungry. This gold will feed them, clothe them and ease their pain.

MARIAN. Sheriff, does Robin Hood speak the truth?

SHERIFF. Marian, my dear, someday you will learn that good money is wasted on the poor.

MARIAN *(appalled)*. Oh! You gross little fever blister! I loathe and despise you! *(To ROBIN.)* Sir, forgive me, will you? I knew not of the vast suffering in my country. And rest assured that upon my return to the kingdom, I shall set forth to contact the King. I will tell him of these unspeakable acts against his people! This, I promise you with all my heart.

SHERIFF. Marian! Do you realize what you're saying is treason against the Prince!

MARIAN. It is not I who have committed treason! *(To ROBIN.)* Do not keep the poor waiting any longer, gallant fugitive. Go, now! But before you do, I have one more treasure for your coffers. *(The MERRY MEN quickly gather closely around ROBIN and MARIAN to ensure they will be a part of this magic moment. They look over ROBIN's and MARIAN's shoulders. MARIAN takes a jeweled ring from her finger and gives it to ROBIN.)* My mother gave me this ring before she died. It will serve her memory well if you use it for your just and noble cause.

MEN *(almost in tears, sighing in unison).* OHHHHHH!

TOWN'S GUY. And it was at this very moment that Robin Hood and the Lady Marian fell in love.

ROBIN *(to AUDIENCE, completely smitten and almost speechless).* Wow!

MARIAN. Now, off with you all! Don't keep those in need waiting a moment longer!

ROBIN. You are the most gracious lady of the land! And I promise you, dear lady, we shall meet again. *(Kisses her hand.)*

MARIAN. I most certainly hope so!

ROBIN. It is time to set forth on our mission! Would you like to join me in my quest to aid the needy, men of Sherwood?

MEN. SURE WOULD!

ROBIN. Very well then…SCATTER! *(Exits, running L.)*

(MEN, screaming, with arms flailing in the air, scatter about, running like maniacs, exiting off L, except for LITTLE JOHN, who exits R.)

MEN. AHHHHHH!!

SHERIFF *(when there's silence)*. Marian! I am appalled by your actions! How could you betray His Highness, the Prince, in this manner?

(LITTLE JOHN, not done scattering yet, runs across stage, screaming, exiting L.)

LITTLE. AHHHHHH!!

SHERIFF *(shoots an annoyed look to LITTLE JOHN as he exits)*. Do you realize that Robin Hood is England's arch-enemy!

MARIAN. No! It is you and the Prince who are the enemies of England! Your time is not long here, Sheriff. The King will hear of your deeds!

SHERIFF. And, dear girl, the Prince shall hear of yours!

(Lights dim and come up on the TOWN'S GUY as MARIAN and the SHERIFF exit.)

TOWN'S GUY. And that's how it all happened. When Marian and the Sheriff returned to the kingdom, Marian made good with her promise. She tried to reach King Richard, but to no avail. Needless to say, THE EVIL PRINCE JOHN…

MEN *(as they enter)*. BOO, HISS! BOO, HISS!

TOWN'S GUY. …was not at all pleased with the recent turn of events.

(During the TOWN'S GUY's next lines, lights slowly come up in Sherwood Forest. ALLAN is sitting playing with a Slinky, having it go back and forth in his hands.

WILL and LITTLE JOHN stare at the Slinky in amazement. ROBIN paces center.)

TOWN'S GUY. When he learned of Marian's allegiance to Robin Hood, he was swift to engage her to the Sheriff of Nottingham, thus securing his position. This now takes us out of the flashback and back to the present time. And so, friends, it seems I'm finished here. I am going back to town. *(To ROBIN.)* WHERE I'M APPRECIATED! *(To AUDIENCE.)* I hope we'll see each other again. Farewell. *(Bows and exits.)*

(Note: Insert additional scene here, found on page 76, if using expanded cast.)

ROBIN. Oh, Friar, what to do, what to do?
TUCK. My son, why don't I go to town to see if there is news. Perhaps an answer to our problem lies there.
ROBIN. Yes, Friar! Be swift on your journey and bring me word of my dear Marian!
TUCK. Yes, my son! *(Exits.)*
ROBIN. Merry Men, we must devise a plan to save Lady Marian before she is forced to wed the Sheriff! Any suggestions, oh quick and clever colleagues?
WILL. Why don't we take our trusty spoons *(all draw their spoons from their sheaths)*, and tunnel into the castle!
MEN *(agreeing to ROBIN)*. YEAH!
ROBIN. How do you propose we do this without the Prince and his guards seeing us?
MEN *(disagreeing voice to WILL)*. Yeah!
WILL. We tunnel from here?
MEN *(agreeing to ROBIN)*. YEAH!

ROBIN. The castle is seventy miles away. By the time we get there, bulldozers will be invented!
MEN *(disagreeing to WILL)*. Yeah! *(MEN put spoons back into sheaths.)*
WILL *(to MEN)*. It was just a thought!
ROBIN. Are there any other stupid suggestions?
LITTLE. Yes, I have one.
ROBIN. Then speak, oh clod.
LITTLE. Why don't we stage a fake fire drill, and when they all run out, we run in!
ALLAN. No! Better yet, let's knock on the door and say we're selling Amway.
WILL. Oh right, who's gonna let in an Amway salesman.
ALLAN. Well, it's better than your stupid tunnel idea!
WILL. Is not!
ALLAN. Is too!
WILL & LITTLE. IS NOT!
ALLAN. IS TOO!
ROBIN *(walks upstage to AUDIENCE, gestures to the MERRY MEN; to AUDIENCE)*. Behold what happens when you drop out of school. ENOUGH! *(He hopelessly sits down and puts his head into his hands.)*

(TOWN'S GUY peers out from behind a tree.)

TOWN'S GUY. Excuse me, I don't mean to be a BOTHER, but I noticed that you're having difficulty getting out of this scene. Might I be of some assistance?
ROBIN *(still with head in his hands)*. Please.
TOWN'S GUY *(sarcastically)*. Oh, my pleasure. *(To AUDIENCE as lights dim.)* While Robin and his Merry Men brainstormed to rescue Lady Marian with the per-

fect plan, the Sheriff and the Prince had been devising a plan of their own.

(Foreboding music. The MERRY MEN turn the tree flats and make up the walls to the throne room and exit. PRINCE JOHN and the FAWNING LADIES enter, the LADIES throw rose petals in PRINCE's path during the TOWN'S GUY's next lines. Once the PRINCE is seated on the throne, the LADIES surround him. One is buffing his nails, the other fanning him, while any others stare at him adoringly.)

TOWN'S GUY. Mr. Technical Director, sweep us to another place in this fair land! You see, the Prince took care of the situation with Marian, but he still had to deal with the problem of Robin Hood. Well, if you thought the Sheriff was nasty, just wait until you meet Prince John. Come with me, good folk, as we witness evil in the making.

(Lights come up on the throne room.)

PRINCE *(to SHERIFF)*. ...and you mean to tell me that Robin Hood intends to lavish the undeserving poor with my royal riches!!
SHERIFF. Yes sir, that's exactly what I mean to say.
PRINCE. Doesn't he know that the poor will just waste the money on something stupid, like—food!
SHERIFF. Feeding the poor, Your Highness, is exactly Robin's intention.
PRINCE. What a fool he is! Two things happen when you feed the poor. Number one: you waste good money.

Number two: you end up with porky poor people. Money has greater purposes in life than feeding the poor!

SHERIFF. He also plans on buying them clothes as well.

PRINCE. Clothes! He wants to buy them clothes! Is the man mad? Have you ever seen a poor person's taste in clothing? They mix rags with burlap and the result is simply a fashion disaster. Do you know that the money Robin Hood stole from me was to go to something really important? *(Points to the window.)* A diamond-studded weather vane for the castle.

FAWNING LADIES *(turn to the window and in unison).* PRETTY!

SHERIFF. How shall you ever get along without it?

PRINCE. I don't know. Thanks to Robin Hood, I shall be weather vane-less and the country will be riddled with poorly appareled, porky poor people! How disheartening. Sheriff, is there nothing to be done to stop this ruffian?

SHERIFF. He's quite hard to keep track of, Your Highness. The forest is so vast that it's impossible to try to find him.

PRINCE. Well then, maybe we could find some way to bring him out in the open to us.

SHERIFF. Impossible! Everything the man wants or needs is in that forest.

PRINCE. Oh come now, certainly there must be something Robin Hood wants that doesn't grow on a tree!

(MARIAN enters.)

MARIAN. I want you to know that I have set every carrier pigeon in England aflight to send my message to the King. He will learn of your treachery and then you will pay! *(Begins to exit, stops.)* I wish you both runny noses! *(Curtsies quickly and exits.)*

SHERIFF *(watches her leave).* Your Highness, I don't think she grew on a tree.

PRINCE. Sheriff, are you thinking what I'm thinking?

PRINCE & SHERIFF *(big evil laughs).* HA, HA, HA, HA!

FAWNING LADIES *(in high-pitched voices, trailing the end of the PRINCE and the SHERIFF's laughs).* Ha, ha, ha, ha, ha! *(One LADY throws a handful of petals in the air.)*

SHERIFF. Yes, but how? How shall we do this?

PRINCE *(takes a moment to think).* I've got it! We will hold an archery tournament!

FAWNING LADIES *(in delight).* OH!

PRINCE. The winner will receive the hand of Lady Marian in marriage and one thousand gold pieces!

FAWNING LADIES *(in delight).* OH!

PRINCE. No doubt Robin Hood will enter! He can win the woman he loves and help the porky poor people at the same time! He won't be able to resist! I'll have all my messengers spread news of the tournament to every inch of the country! Word will be sure to reach the outlaw and his men! And the best part is, we don't have to worry about him winning! As we all know, *you* are the best archer in all the land. You have a perfect record, never to have been beaten by anyone!

SHERIFF *(modestly).* It's a gift.

PRINCE. This is perfect! This is brilliant! Oh, I love me! *(FAWNING LADIES applaud. The PRINCE blows them a kiss.)*

FAWNING LADIES *(as they "catch" the imaginary kiss).* OH!

SHERIFF. Your Highness, I just ask one thing of you as reward for my actions.

PRINCE. Name it, oh faithful Sheriff.

SHERIFF. I want Robin Hood present at the wedding. I want him in chains, watching me marry his love, completely helpless to stop it. Then, after we cut the cake…

FAWNING LADIES *(big smiles)*. CAKE!

SHERIFF. I want Robin Hood beheaded. You might say it's a surprise wedding gift for the bride. Wish me a runny nose, will she?

PRINCE. Oh, Sheriff, how absolutely ghastly. A beheading! I like it! Oh, you and I are a fine team. *(Shakes SHERIFF's hand.)* Robin will come out of hiding, he will be captured, you will marry Marian, I will dethrone my brother Richard, become king AND ENGLAND WILL BE OURS! We will rule this country as we please! The people of England will do as we command or die! What a fun place to live this shall be! Oh, joy! Oh, elation! Oh, goodie!

(The PRINCE and SHERIFF laugh as FAWNING LADIES throw rose petals. PRINCE, SHERIFF and LADIES exit. Lights come up on the TOWN'S GUY as MERRY MEN turn the flats to change back to Sherwood Forest.)

TOWN'S GUY. Pretty dramatic, huh? I do say, those are two nasty people! Prince John spread word throughout the land about the archery tournament. As news reached the forest, Robin and his men were still figuring out a plan to rescue Marian.

Act I   ROBIN HOOD   25

(Lights come up in Sherwood Forest. ROBIN is sitting with his head in his hands as the MERRY MEN keep trying to think of plans.)

ALLAN. No, wait...and then...get this, this is really good...and then we show up with champagne, balloons and this big fake check for a million dollars, and we tell him he's just won the Publisher's Clearing House Sweepstakes and...

ROBIN *(can take it no longer)*. STOP IT! JUST STOP IT! *(As FRIAR TUCK enters.)* Don't think of a plan! I'll think of a plan! Just...don't think of a plan.

TUCK. Robin! I've just come from the kingdom! Men... *(Holds up a large box of Yodels—a brand of cake.)*

MEN *(see the box; in unison to AUDIENCE)*. YODELS!! *(They run to FRIAR, grabbing box.)*

ROBIN. Have you news for me, Friar?

TUCK. Have I ever! Look! *(Hands ROBIN a parchment announcement. Joins MEN.)*

ROBIN. Men, listen! *(Reads.)* "His Royal Highness hereby decrees an archery tournament shall take place one week from this Saturday. The winner shall receive one thousand pieces of gold and the hand of Lady Marian in marriage. Entries must be postmarked by Sunday, void where prohibited by law." Merry Men, I have a plan! I shall enter this archery tournament! No doubt I shall win, for as we all know, I am the best archer in the land! I shall win the tournament, marry Lady Marian and give the gold to the poor people!

MEN *(with their mouths full of Yodels)*. GEE, ROBIN! WHAT A GREAT PLAN!

ROBIN. Yes, I thought you'd like it. *(Waves to MEN in triumph.)* Huzzah, huzzah! Now, there is work to be done! First, I must practice my archery. For after all, even someone who's the very best must work hard and practice every day to stay that way. *(Looks to AUDIENCE, points to them and says quickly:)* Did you all get that? Good. *(To the MEN.)* Let the training begin!

ALLAN. Begin training now, Robin? But it's pitch black! It's ten-thirty at night!

ROBIN. What better time to begin than now! *(Hands a piece of burlap with a target to WILL.)* Will, hurry to yon hawthorn! I say unto you hence, be my herald, hasten hither. Haste makes waste for henceforth lies hereafter! Hither and yon is but hence hitherto. So hereby, hindrance shall make a heedless hazard! So be not heathen, hurry, hero, and hasten hither hence. Huzzah!

WILL *(stares at him a moment)*. I have no idea what you've just said.

ROBIN *(sighs; points offstage)*. Do you see that tree over there?

WILL. Yes.

ROBIN. Stick this on it.

WILL. Thank you. Why couldn't you say that in the first place?

ROBIN *(calls after him)*. Excuse me, it's called the art of language! Allan, my bow and arrow! *(ALLAN hands him the bow and arrow.)* And now, would you like to watch me as I strike a bull's-eye for justice, men of Sherwood?

MEN. SURE WOULD! *(ROBIN picks up his bow, puts an arrow to it and aims it offstage.)*

TOWN'S GUY. Robin practiced morning, noon and night. And as the men were soon to find out, his aim was much better morning and noon than it was at night. *(ROBIN shoots an imaginary arrow offstage and we hear a scream.)*

WILL *(offstage)*. AHHHHHH!

ROBIN. Will, are you all right?

WILL *(offstage)*. Fine, boss! I always wanted to get my ear pierced.

ROBIN. Well then, glad to be of help! *(Waves to him.)* Huzzah, huzzah!

LITTLE. Ohhh. I'll get the Band-aids. *(MERRY MEN exit, running to WILL's aid.)*

TOWN'S GUY. Yes, Robin was indeed the best archer in all the land…during the day. But as the days passed, he could not help but think how worried his dear Marian must be with the recent turn of events.

ROBIN. You know, as the days pass, I cannot help but think how worried my dear Marian must be with the recent turn of events.

TOWN'S GUY. He thought he should go to her and reassure her that he will win the tournament and everyone will live happily ever after.

ROBIN. I think I should go to her and reassure her that I will win the tournament and everyone will live happily ever after.

TOWN'S GUY. Robin, I don't think you're getting the whole concept of the narrator, are you? You see, the point of me telling the audience these things is so you don't have to.

ROBIN. Yes, but that would give you more lines then me. And as we all know, this play is called "The Somewhat True Tale of Robin Hood." Not *(gives a little laugh)* "The Somewhat True Tale of the Town's Guy." This

isn't rocket science here. *(Gives him a little punch in the arm.)* Now, if you will, have your technical friend take us to the Lady Marian.
TOWN'S GUY. Of course, sir. Mr. Technical Director, if you please, transport my valiant friend, AND HIS ENORMOUS EGO, to the chamber of Lady Marian. *(Exits.)*
ROBIN *(as he follows the TOWN'S GUY)*. I don't have an enormous ego. I just happen to know I'm the most important person in this play. *(Exits.)*

(The MERRY MEN turn the flats to form MARIAN's chamber. The sets are arranged so there is a doorway and a large window. The room is stark except for a chair and a dress dummy which has MARIAN's wedding gown on it. The wedding gown should be full-length to the floor and have long sleeves. The dummy should not have a head or arms.)

LADY *(holds veil)*. But try this on. You'll look lovely, my lady.
MARIAN. Oh, who cares. Soon I shall be forced to marry a festering wart. That will make me Mrs. Festering Wart. Then, he and I shall have a passel of festering little warts. On our mailbox it will say "The Warts" and our Christmas cards will be signed, "Brightest Holiday Greetings, the Wart Family." So who cares how I look, I have nothing to live for. *(Plops herself down in the chair.)*
LADY *(puts veil on dummy)*. Somebody's cranky. *(There is a "boink" sound that indicates an arrow has just been shot into the outside of the window. The LADY goes to the window, pulls out the arrow that has a letter at-*

tached to it. She shows it to MARIAN.) Oh, Lady Marian, a letter has just arrived for you...air-row mail. *(Laughs hysterically at her own joke, looks at MARIAN, gets no response.)* Boy, when you're having a bad hair day, the whole world suffers.

MARIAN. Please do read it, Lady.

LADY. As you wish. "Let it be known that His Royal Highness, hereby decrees an archery tournament shall take place one week from this Saturday. All eligible archers are commanded to take part. The winner shall receive one thousand gold pieces and the hand of Lady Marian in marriage."

MARIAN. What! Let me see that. *(LADY hands her the letter.)*

LADY. This is wonderful! You may not have to marry the Sheriff of Nottingham after all!

MARIAN. Don't let this fool you, Lady. This is just a clever ploy by THE EVIL PRINCE JOHN.

MEN *(offstage)*. BOO, HISS! BOO, HISS! *(LADY looks around in confusion to see where the "Boo Hiss" came from.)*

MARIAN. Now he can justify my hand in marriage to the Sheriff. The Sheriff is by far the best archer in all the land. His record is perfect, he's never been beaten by anyone. He is sure to win. This way, it will look all quite innocent to the people of England when the Sheriff elects the Prince king. Nothing has changed, I'm still doomed. *(Plops herself down in the chair. Hands LADY the arrow and message.)*

(ROBIN HOOD appears in the window. He waves to the LADY.)

LADY *(spotting ROBIN).* Why, Lady Marian, there's a Robin on the windowsill.

MARIAN *(stands and sees ROBIN).* Oh, look! It's Robin Hood! Bold and courageous desperado of Sherwood and reputable defender of the underfed!

(ROBIN enters the room.)

LADY *(to ROBIN).* Well, I see we're into titles.

MARIAN. Lady, will you stand watch outside my door? If the good outlaw Robin Hood is found in my chamber, there could be an unpleasant situation.

LADY *(to MARIAN).* I don't like the sound of this.

ROBIN. You can trust in me, good lady.

LADY. Yes, sir. *(To MARIAN.)* I still don't like the sound of this. *(Exits with arrow and message. MARIAN and ROBIN shyly smile at each other.)*

MARIAN. So, Robin, how art thou?

ROBIN. Very well. And…how art thou?

MARIAN. Oh, I art fine. Well, actually, I'm about to become Mrs. Wart, but aside from that, I art fine.

ROBIN. Good. Did you receive my message?

MARIAN. Oh! That was from you?

ROBIN. Yes! Good news to you, no doubt.

MARIAN. Oh, don't be fooled, Robin! This is just a scheme to deceive the people of England. The Sheriff is the best archer in all the land. He will win and I will be condemned to marry him. All is black and my dreams, once bright, spiral into the murky abyss of misery, despondency and tragic woe. *(Upbeat with a smile.)* But thanks for asking anyway. *(Plops herself down in the chair.)*

ROBIN. My dear damsel in distress, you have been deceived. The Sheriff is indeed a master archer, but he is only the *second* best in all the land. Stands before you now, the winner of the tournament and your future husband.

MARIAN. You? The greatest archer in the land?

ROBIN. Well, Marian, I am not a person who likes to brag…

MEN *(offstage)*. YEAH, RIGHT!

ROBIN *(shoots a nasty look offstage)*. …but when it comes to archery, there is no man better than me! With my trusty bow and arrow, I can split a pea, on the back of a flea, five hundred feet away! *(Under his breath.)* As long as it's during daylight.

MARIAN. Can this be? Is there hope for happiness yet?

ROBIN. Yes, my love, 'tis true. There is hope for happiness yet.

(They draw close about to kiss as the LADY IN WAITING bursts into the room.)

LADY *(in a panic, screams)*. LADY MARIAN!

ROBIN *(annoyed)*. Timing, dear girl. You must work on your timing.

LADY. But this is urgent! Robin's been seen! The Sheriff and his guards are searching the castle and they're headed this way. *(Grabs ROBIN's arm and tugs away at him.)* OH, WHAT SHALL WE DO?

ROBIN *(as he's being shaken)*. Prozac comes to mind!*

MARIAN. Robin, if you are found it will mean certain death for us all!

---

* This line may be cut if questionable to be performed by a school or young cast.

LADY. Whoa. Wait just a fortnight. Nobody said anything to me about death when I took this job.

MARIAN. Lady, please, there is no time. Watch for the Sheriff. Quick, Robin, to the window!

LADY *(throws her arms in the air)*. I knew this was going to happen! Did I listen to my parents and go to law school? NOOOOO! I had to be a big shot working at the castle!

ROBIN *(begins to climb out the window)*. Oh no! The guards are below!

LADY *(to ROBIN)*. "You can trust in me, good lady." And what good did it do me? Thanks to you, I'm gonna be floatin' in a moat somewhere!

ROBIN. Are you quite finished?

LADY. Oh, I'm just getting started!

ROBIN. Marian, I must find a place to hide! *(Looks around searching for a place to hide. Notices there is no place. He picks up the small chair and holds it in front of his face.)*

LADY *(at the doorway)*. Lady Marian, the Sheriff's one chamber over! Oh my heart. My heart is giving out.

ROBIN *(realizing this will not be inconspicuous, puts the chair down)*. Something tells me when playing hide and seek, this is not the first room one chooses.

LADY *(panics; looks out the doorway)*. LADY MARIAN, THE SHERIFF APPROACHES!

MARIAN. Quick, Robin, stand behind here! *(Points to dummy. ROBIN stands behind the dummy and puts his head on the dummy's neck. MARIAN puts the veil on ROBIN's head.)*

Act I ROBIN HOOD 33

LADY. OHHHHH! I'M DYING! I'M DYING! *(Looks up and talks to heaven.)* What's that, Grandma? Come toward the light?
MARIAN. Lady, help!

(The SHERIFF and GUARDS, wearing black tunics and black hoods with the eyes cut out of them, burst into the room.)

SHERIFF. All right, Marian! Where is he?
MARIAN. Doesn't thou even knowest enough to knock? What were thou brought up in…a barn?
SHERIFF. Don't play coy with me. I'm on to your tricks. That blackguard, Robin Hood, has been seen about the castle. My sources say he was scaling the wall to your window.
MARIAN. I have no idea what you mean, you walking, talking skin abrasion.
SHERIFF. Why on earth do you insist on protecting him? Please, what could you possibly see in that loser? *(ROBIN looks at the SHERIFF and puts his hands [holding the sleeves of the wedding gown] on his hips in disgust at that remark.)* I mean, think about it. He's completely uncivilized. The man lives in the woods. His entire social circle consists of field mice and ticks. *(Stands closer to the dummy.)* However, your future could be quite bright with someone like me, my sweet. You'd have wealth beyond your grandest dreams! But taking up with the likes of Robin Hood would mean you'd have to live a life below you. *(Stands directly next to ROBIN.)* You would be one of the vile and worthless poor. And

they're not fit to be spat upon by someone of our stature!

ROBIN. THAT DID IT! *(He grabs the SHERIFF by the throat and begins to choke him.)*

SHERIFF. AHHHHHH! HELP! *(ROBIN chokes him for a second, then, throws him to the ground.)*

ROBIN *(forgetting he's still wearing the veil, delivers these lines very intensely).* So! The poor are not fit for you to spit upon! For shame! It is evil hearts like yours that keep the poor in the throes of their deep oppression!

MARIAN *(out of the corner of her mouth to ROBIN).* Robin, I think this will play much better if you lose the veil.

ROBIN. Oh, right. Thank you. *(Hands her the veil, goes back to the monologue. To SHERIFF.)* How dare you make fun of those less fortunate than you! It is no crime to be poor! But, it *is* a crime to be a thief! You and the Prince took away their money, then you took away their homes. And now you mock them! It is what's inside someone's heart that really matters! One person is no better than another person merely because they have money! *(Looks to AUDIENCE, points to them, and says quickly.)* Did you all get that? Good.

SHERIFF. Enough of your nonsense! *(To GUARDS.)* Arrest him! *(GUARDS approach ROBIN.)*

ROBIN. AH HA! *(Draws his spoon from his sheath. The GUARDS gasp.)*

GUARD 1. Stand back! He's got a spoon! *(They take a step back.)*

SHERIFF *(grabs MARIAN by the arm and holds a knife to her).* Yes. And I have a knife! May I suggest you surrender, sir. We wouldn't want things to get messy, would we?

MARIAN. Robin, don't worry about me! Escape and continue your crusade for the poor!
SHERIFF. Oh, you are a sappy one, aren't you? *(ROBIN drops his spoon. SHERIFF releases MARIAN. To GUARDS.)* Arrest him! *(GUARDS take ROBIN into custody.)*

(PRINCE enters with FAWNING LADIES throwing rose petals.)

PRINCE. What goes on here?!
SHERIFF. We have an unwelcome visitor, Your Highness.
PRINCE. Can it be? Why it is! It's Robin Hood! Felon, lawbreaker and partisan of the poorly appareled, porky poor people. Well, dear fellow, it looks as though we are about to defeat your crusade for the underprivileged, now, doesn't it?
ROBIN. You've only won the battle, sir, not the war!
PRINCE. You're not going to be in any condition to battle anyone. Guards! Take Robin Hood to—THE DUNGEON OF DEMISE!
LADY *(screams in terror).* AHHHHHH! *(Then, completely composes herself. As the LADY screams the PRINCE, SHERIFF and FAWNING LADIES almost go into cardiac arrest. One FAWNING LADY looks at the LADY IN WAITING and throws a handful of rose petals at her in anger. All compose themselves and the action continues.)*
PRINCE. Sheriff, have you any suggestions as to the torture for a criminal the likes of him?
SHERIFF. I say, whip him!
FAWNING LADIES. Oh!
PRINCE. Too nice.

SHERIFF. Brand him with irons!
FAWNING LADIES. Oh!
PRINCE. Too nice.
SHERIFF. Cut out his tongue!
FAWNING LADIES. Eew!
PRINCE. Messy! And too nice. Wait, I think I've got it! *(Evil laugh.)*
SHERIFF. Why, Your Highness—you don't mean?
PRINCE. Yes! Let us see if our gallant hero can survive spending Christmas with... *(Pulls out CD.)* Kathie Lee.*
LADY *(screams in terror)*. AHHHHHH! *(Then, completely composes herself.)*
SHERIFF *(covers his ear with his hand and looks at the LADY)*. I hate you.
MARIAN. NO! PLEASE! NOT THAT!
ROBIN *(coldly to the PRINCE)*. Your heart is black!
PRINCE. Thank you!
MARIAN *(to PRINCE)*. No wait! Please, you cannot do this! What would be my life without Robin Hood! *(Very dramatically.)* There would be no sunshine, for there would be no morning. There would be no dreams come true, for there would be no more stars to wish upon. Happiness would just be a memory. *(Building to a climax.)* I tell you, sir, spare him and you spare my heart and my soul. I cannot go on without him! Please! Please! I beg you! Don't take him away! NO!!

(MARIAN collapses in tears as the rest of the cast looks at her blankly for a second, then applauds her. ROBIN breaks away from the GUARD, takes MARIAN's hand,

---

* If Kathie Lee is no longer *en vogue* you may substitute the goofball *du jour*.

leads her center stage. She takes a bow to AUDIENCE, as the cast still applauds her. The TOWN'S GUY enters with a bouquet of roses. He hands them to her, then joins the cast in applauding her.)

SHERIFF. ALL RIGHT, ENOUGH! Brilliantly played, Marian, but your pleas fall on deaf ears. *(Points to GUARD.)* Have someone posted outside the door at all times! I want to make sure she stays where she belongs!

GUARD. Yes, sir!

PRINCE. Sheriff, I want you be in charge of the excruciating torture and demise of Robin Hood.

SHERIFF. Why, Your Highness, you're too kind!

PRINCE. Look at it as part of the festivities for your bachelor party. *(To MARIAN.)* And most grooms-to-be only get a handmaiden popping out of a cake! *(Laughs coldly in her face and exits with the FAWNING LADIES following, throwing rose petals.)*

SHERIFF. Guards, start the torture immediately. Then, after his brain has turned to Jello, tie him up, stuff him in a sack and throw him in the river! Now...take this trash out of here! *(He laughs coldly as the GUARDS exit with ROBIN. MARIAN collapses in grief in the chair.)* Don't cry too hard, dear girl. I don't want to have a puffy-eyed bride.

MARIAN. Monster! May unsightly dandruff curse your head and the heads of those who love you! *(The SHERIFF laughs and exits.)* Oh, my poor Robin Hood! What a ghastly fate he faces! And here am I, held captive in my chamber, unable to help him! Oh, can anything be done to save him? *(MARIAN puts her head down and cries quietly. THE LADY IN WAITING, with her back to the audience, tends to the wedding dress and veil.)*

TOWN'S GUY. Excuse me, Lady Marian, forgive me for being so bold, but maybe I can be of some assistance.

MARIAN *(stares at him a moment)*. I don't mean to be rude, but who on earth are you?

TOWN'S GUY. I'm the Town's Guy.

MARIAN. The Town's Guy? Oh yes, you're that lovely chap from the flashback.

TOWN'S GUY. Yes, that's me.

MARIAN. How very good to see you again.

TOWN'S GUY. Thank you.

MARIAN. Do tell me, good Town's Guy, can anything be done to save my dear Robin?

TOWN'S GUY. I shall go to Sherwood Forest and tell the Merry Men that Robin has been captured. Together, we will devise a plan to rescue him!

MARIAN. A worthy thought. But alas, there isn't enough time! Sherwood Forest is well over seventy miles away! By the time you get there and back, it will be too late!

TOWN'S GUY. Not necessarily. Tell me, have you ever heard of…fade out and segue to next scene?

MARIAN. No, I can't say that I have.

TOWN'S GUY. Well, it's this wonderful effect I can achieve with the help of my friend *(points out into the dark)*, Mr. Technical Director. *(Waves to the technical director. MARIAN joins TOWN'S GUY in waving. Then out of the corner of her mouth:)*

MARIAN. I don't see anyone.

TOWN'S GUY. Trust me, he's out there. With his help, I can be transported to Sherwood Forest in a flash! Then, in another flash, the Merry Men and I will be on our way to rescue Robin Hood!

MARIAN. Splendid! Good Town's Guy, waste not another moment of precious time! You and your fine friend get to work! *(Waves to the technical director.)*

TOWN'S GUY. Thank you, my lady.

MARIAN. No, thank you!

TOWN'S GUY. Mr. Technical Director, if you please! Do do that voodoo that you do so well!

(Lights fade. The MERRY MEN enter and change scene to Sherwood Forest.)

MARIAN *(as lights fade)*. Oh! Oh! This is so exciting! I've never faded out before!

(MARIAN exits. The MERRY MEN take their places, center. The LADY IN WAITING, oblivious to what is happening, still tends to the veil and dress.)

TOWN'S GUY. And now, good folk, it's back to Sherwood Forest we go! I will tell the Merry Men of Robin's capture. Then, Mr. Technical Director and I will lead them to Robin Hood and save the day! My journey was swift and I was amongst the trees in no time!

(Lights come up in Sherwood Forest. THE LADY IN WAITING is standing in the middle of the MERRY MEN.)

LADY *(to herself with her back to AUDIENCE)*. I coulda been a teacher. I coulda been a stockbroker. Heck, even retail is better than this! *(The TOWN'S GUY taps her on* the shoulder. She looks at him blankly, then realizes where she is.) Oh my gosh! I forgot to fade! Ahhh… *(Pause.)* BYE! *(Grabs dress dummy, exits, running offstage.)*

TOWN'S GUY. Merry Men, your attention please! *(The MEN quickly gather round him. The TOWN'S GUY takes a long look at the MERRY MEN and notices they're all wearing earrings. The earrings should be pretty large and noticeable by the AUDIENCE as well. I give you full license to be silly.)* Ah…what's with the earrings?

LITTLE *(points to his earrings)*. Evening target practice, sir.

ALLAN. Robin hasn't quite perfected his aim in the black of night yet.

WILL. Yeah, and if you think we look funny, you should see the horses.

TUCK *(to TOWN'S GUY)*. Sir, our leader, Robin Hood, has not returned from his journey. We fear something terrible has happened to him. Have you any news?

TOWN'S GUY. I do, Friar. Robin Hood has been captured and imprisoned in…the Dungeon of Demise!

(LADY enters, running.)

LADY *(screams in terror)*. AHHHHHH! *(Exits running.)*

TUCK. Lord have mercy on Robin! What a horrible place the Dungeon of Demise is!

WILL. I'll say! It's worse than Motor Vehicle[*].

TOWN'S GUY. And there, Robin may meet with a most horrible fate if we don't help him! Good men of Sherwood, we must begin our quest to fade out and segue to the palace!

---

[*] May be changed to D.M.V. (Department of Motor Vehicles) or whatever name your state's motor vehicle department is called.

TUCK. Yes! Let us band together to save our commander in chief, Robin Hood!
MEN *(to AUDIENCE, in unison)*. YES! TO SAVE ROBIN HOOD!
TUCK *(as lights dim)*. I pray we will reach him in time!
TOWN'S GUY. I, too, good Friar. But who knows, IT MAY ALREADY BE TOO LATE! Men, huddle together! *(Out to the technical director.)* Mr. Technical Director, with truth and justice at your side, send to us to our hero, Robin Hood!
MEN *(as lights begin to flicker)*. WHOOOOAAAA!

(Lights FADE on MEN as they exit and come up on the Dungeon of Demise. The flat has a prison window with bars on it. There is a sign on the flat that reads THE DUNGEON OF DEMISE. ROBIN appears in the window.)

ROBIN. Prince John and the Sheriff will not defeat me! I will escape. Then, I will save Lady Marian and rescue the poor! I CAN DO THIS FOR I AM GOOD! AND BECAUSE I AM GOOD, I WILL NOT BE BEATEN! THERE IS NOTHING IN THIS WORLD THAT CAN STOP ME!!

(Music starts, and a woman's voice—which is loud and far too perky—fades in singing the last verse of "The Twelve Days of Christmas."*)

---

* The most effective way to achieve the Kathie Lee song is to have someone sing it to a karaoke recording or piano accompaniment. Music should still be played under the Prince's and Sheriff's last lines. You may substitute this song with something equally obnoxious concerning the recent beat-to-death fad of the day. In the past, Robin Hood has been "Titaniced," "Hasoned," "Brady Bunched" and "Spice Girled" to death. You may change it as long as good taste prevails.

KATHIE LEE. "On the twelfth day of Christmas my true love gave to me…"

ROBIN. Oh no! *(Looks around in horror.)*

KATHIE LEE *(quickly)*. "Twelve drummers drumming, eleven pipers piping, ten lords a-leaping, nine ladies dancing, eight maids a-milking, seven swans a-swimming, six geese a-laying…" *(Music gradually getting louder.)*

ROBIN. NO!

KATHIE LEE. "Five golden rings…"

ROBIN *(pulls on bars trying to escape; out into AUDIENCE)*. NOT THIS!!

(Music swells, the lights come up on PRINCE JOHN and the SHERIFF. The SHERIFF holds a champagne bottle and he and PRINCE JOHN both hold champagne glasses.)

KATHIE LEE, PRINCE & SHERIFF. "Four calling birds, three French hens, two turtle doves…AND A PARTRIDGE IN A PEAR TREE!"

PRINCE. Happy holidays, Robin Hood!

SHERIFF. And God bless us, everyone!

ROBIN *(covers his ears and slowly sinks below the window)*. AHHHHHH!!

(PRINCE JOHN and the SHERIFF laugh and toast each other. On the last chord of music—blackout.)

END OF ACT ONE

ACT TWO

(Prior to curtain a recording of the overly perky woman's voice singing, "Deck the Halls" is played. The curtain rises as the song fades out and the action starts immediately after the music stops.)

SCENE: *Outside the Dungeon of Demise. There is no sign of ROBIN HOOD.*

AT RISE: *As lights come up, the TOWN'S GUY and MERRY MEN fade in. Note: The MERRY MEN are no longer wearing earrings.*

MEN. WHOOOOAAAA!! *(When lights are up full, they break from the huddle.)*
WILL. Wow! This was too cool!
LITTLE. I'll say! I like fading out much better than flashing back.
ALLAN. No way! Flashbacks are much better than fading out.
LITTLE. Are not!
ALLAN. Are too!
LITTLE. Are not!
ALLAN. Are too!
TUCK. My sons, please! To our task at hand.

TOWN'S GUY *(points to dungeon)*. Look! It's the Dungeon of Demise!

(LADY enters, screams, sends half the MERRY MEN to drop for cover, the other half in cardiac arrest.)

LADY. AHHHHHH! *(Looks at MEN, sees she's knocked them down. Big smile to AUDIENCE, raises one arm in the air in triumph.)* YES! *(Exits running.)*

ALLAN. Town's Guy, where is our fearless leader?

TOWN'S GUY *(listens at the prison window)*. Men! Over here! I think I hear something! *(Hears some incoherent muttering.)* Robin Hood of Sherwood Forest, are you in there?!

(ROBIN pulls himself up and is seen in the window.)

ROBIN *(in a dazed and weak voice)*. "Seven swans a-swimming, six geese a-laying, five golden rings…"

ALLAN. Wow. He's bonkers!

TUCK. Robin Hood of Sherwood Forest, can you hear me?

ROBIN *(looks at FRIAR TUCK confused)*. Regis…is that you?[*]

TUCK. Robin! It's me! Friar Tuck.

ROBIN. Cody, Cody, Cody, Cody, Cody, Cody…[*]

TUCK. Robin, snap out of it so you can battle the Sheriff and THE EVIL PRINCE JOHN…

---

[*] If you have changed the song used at the end of Act I, Robin's two lines about Regis and Cody are not appropriate. You may adjust these lines to coincide with whatever form of torture you use. Please note that you are only allowed to change these two lines.

MEN *(to AUDIENCE, quickly in unison).* BOO, HISS! BOO, HISS!

WILL. Snap out of it so you can combat tyranny and injustice!

ALLAN. Snap out of it so you can restore integrity to the throne!

LITTLE. Snap out of it so you can re-open the mall! *(The MEN look at LITTLE JOHN.)* Okay, so don't buy your tights at The Gap and see how long they last.

TOWN'S GUY. Robin, you must save the poor from suffering and starvation!

ROBIN *(looks at TOWN'S GUY, then in a weak voice).* The poor…the poor, they're starving… *(Coming out of it as his voice is getting stronger.)* I must help the poor.

TOWN'S GUY. And Lady Marian!

ROBIN *(voice strong).* Yes! I must save the poor and Lady Marian from certain doom!

TOWN'S GUY. YES, ROBIN!

ROBIN *(back to his boastful self).* I must prevail and set this land free from dictatorship! I can do this because I am Robin Hood! I am the conqueror of evil and exemplar of good! I am THE ULTIMATE HERO!

TOWN'S GUY *(to AUDIENCE).* Guess who just found his ego.

TUCK *(to TOWN'S GUY).* Yes, Town's Guy! He is truly pompous! *(To AUDIENCE.)* OUR LEADER IS BACK!

MEN *(to AUDIENCE, in unison).* HOORAY! *(The MEN cheer as ROBIN waves victoriously to them through the bars.)*

ROBIN. Yes, thank you! Huzzah, huzzah! Now, get me out of here!

TUCK. But, Robin, my son, the walls are concrete! However can we hope to free you?
ROBIN. Town's Guy *(points into AUDIENCE)*, is your director friend still out there somewhere?
TOWN'S GUY. Yes, Robin, he is.
ROBIN. Splendid! *(Out to the technical director.)* Stand by, good sir! Your skills are needed! *(To MEN.)* Merry Men, gather round! You must all listen very carefully! I HAVE A PLAN! *(All gather under the window and make muddle sounds as if discussing the "plan.")* Get it?
MEN *(in unison)*. GOT IT!
ROBIN. Good! Now, would you like to help me, as I set my ingenious plan to work, men of Sherwood?
MEN *(in unison)*. SURE WOULD!
ROBIN. Very well then...SCATTER!

(Blackout. The MEN are screaming and running all over the place. There should be very strange sound effects during the blackout, such as: a jackhammer, chickens squawking, a train signal, a cow mooing, a car horn, etc. Note: The blackout should be quick. When lights come up full, ROBIN and EVERYONE, except LITTLE JOHN, are standing completely composed in front of the Dungeon of Demise.)

MEN *(in unison)*. GEE, ROBIN, WHAT A GREAT PLAN!
ROBIN. Yes, I thought you'd like it.

(LITTLE JOHN, still scattering, runs on stage screaming, his hands waving frantically.)

LITTLE. AHHHHHH!

ROBIN. John! I'm out.
LITTLE *(completely composed)*. Oh. Okay. *(Stands with other MEN.)*
ROBIN. Men, we must hurry back to Sherwood Forest! I must prepare for the archery tournament tomorrow!
MEN *(cheer in unison)*. HOORAY!
ROBIN. I must be in tiptop shape to win the gold for the poor and the hand of Lady Marian.
MEN *(cheer in unison)*. HOORAY!
ROBIN. Therefore, I must practice all day...
MEN *(cheer in unison)*. HOORAY!
ROBIN. And I must practice all night!
MEN *(unenthusiastically, under their breath)*. "Ow. Not again. My ears can't take this." *(One man rubs his earlobe.)*
ROBIN. Soon, this nightmare will be over and England will be safe again! Are you ready, Merry Men?
MEN *(in unison)*. READY, ROBIN!
ROBIN. Very well then...SCATTER! *(The MEN scream and run, their arms flailing in the air. The Dungeon of Demise flat should slide offstage. ROBIN and the MEN exit.)*
TOWN'S GUY. And as Robin and his team headed back to Sherwood Forest, plans were being made for the social event of the decade.

(The throne room flats should be brought on and set in place for the next scene.)

TOWN'S GUY. The Prince and Sheriff were quite confident that they had everything well under control. They thought wrong! As you will see, they were not expecting some surprise news from the Lady Marian.

(TOWN'S GUY exits. Lights up on the throne room. PRINCE JOHN sits on his throne and the SHERIFF stands next to him with a clipboard in his hands. The FAWNING LADIES are sitting. One is reading a magazine, one is meditating, one is painting her toenails and another is plucking her eyebrows.)

Sitting w/ legs over side of chair   Nick on R side

PRINCE. Oh Sheriff, Sheriff, it will not be long now. Soon, I shall become king and England will be all ours!

(LITTLE JOHN, still scattering, runs across stage screaming, and off, behind the flats, his arms are flailing as usual. He should be "outside the castle" and able to be seen through the windows in the flats.)

run from UL down stairs, pause in front of throne, keep running

follow him with your eyes, pause

LITTLE. AHHHHHH! *(The PRINCE and SHERIFF look at him as he passes, they pause a moment.)*

PRINCE. Who was that?

SHERIFF. I don't know. But that was quite a feat considering we're in a tower. But, as you were saying, Highness, I agree! It looks as though all our hard work is about to pay off! *(FAWNING LADIES applaud with glee.)*

GUARD. Excuse me, Your Highness! Urgent news! Robin Hood has escaped! enter UR, come on only slightly

FAWNING LADIES *(gasp). Oh!* — cross over towards guard

SHERIFF. What! The knave escaped! This cannot be!

PRINCE. Guard, bring the Lady Marian to me at once. still laying/sitting

GUARD. Yes, Your Highness. *(Exits.)* — Exit UR

Act II ROBIN HOOD 49

PRINCE. Worry not, Sheriff! You know he'll be here tomorrow for the archery tournament. And mark my words, he will be captured. We just have to take the proper precautions to make the Lady Marian remain extremely unavailable to him.

(MARIAN and GUARD enter.)

MARIAN. You sent for me, oh pimple on the face of humanity?

PRINCE. Yes, Marian, I sent for you. Robin Hood has escaped.

MARIAN. Oh rapture and extreme satisfaction! Robin Hood, holder of my heart, free! Now, he will surely rescue me and save me from the evil clutches of *(to PRINCE and SHERIFF)* Scab-King and his faithful sidekick, Blotch.

PRINCE. Don't count on it, dear girl. Until the tournament tomorrow, you will stay here, in the tower, heavily guarded at all times. We must see to it that you marry the Sheriff so I can become king!

SHERIFF *(with evil glee in his voice)*. Yes, darling, it will be a grand party. All the most important people in the world will be our guests. See, I have the seating arrangements for the reception right here. *(Hands her the clipboard.)*

MARIAN *(glances at the clipboard)*. Oh, for goodness sakes, can't you do anything right? Look at the people at table three.

SHERIFF *(looks over her shoulder at clipboard)*. What's wrong with table three?

MARIAN. You've got Genghis Khan sitting next to the Pope. Oh, that'll go over real big.

SHERIFF. Then where do you suggest I put him? *-get idea*

MARIAN. Well…Genghis Khan is a barbarian whose face strikes fear in the hearts of men. Sit him next to your sister…they'll have a lot in common!

SHERIFF. Don't pick on my sister! *-Walk back to throne R side*

PRINCE. So as you see, dear niece, you haven't a choice. All the final preparations have been made for the wedding. *(PRINCE points to FAWNING LADIES. With big smiles, three hold up white, accordion paper wedding bells and one holds up a "JUST MARRIED" sign.)* go back to

MARIAN *(to LADIES)*. I wish you all…split ends. throne

FAWNING LADIES *(in horror, they drop their bells and grab their hair)*. AHHHHHHH!

PRINCE. Appreciate our hard work! You and the Sheriff will be wed the moment after he wins the archery tournament! *-walk to Ledge*

MARIAN. Well yes, I imagine that would be your idea of a happy ending. But you and the Sheriff have overlooked one small detail. The Sheriff is only the *second* best archer in all the land. It is Robin Hood who is the very best archer in all the land. Why, five hundred feet away, he can split a hair growing out of a crusty mole on your little toe!

SHERIFF. What is it with you and skin conditions? *-still by throne*

MARIAN. Robin Hood will defeat you! Then, England will once again belong to the people. And boy, oh, boy, are they going to be mad at you! *-walk over to Prince*

PRINCE. NO MORE! GUARD, TAKE HER AWAY! *-yell, stand*

MARIAN. May you both itch in places you cannot reach! *(Curtsies and exits with GUARD.)* *-Exit UR*

Act II ROBIN HOOD 51

Stand walk forward

PRINCE. Curses! Curses! Robin Hood the best archer in all the land! *walk to him*

SHERIFF. She's lying, Your Highness! Let the tournament take place. I'm sure I can beat him.

PRINCE. No, Sheriff! *slap* We cannot risk it! Everything we have accomplished is at stake! If Robin Hood wins, we are doomed! We must think of another plan. *(Looks at the SHERIFF a moment.)* Tell me, what else are you good at? *forward* *back to him*

SHERIFF. Gee, I don't know offhand.

PRINCE. Can you fence?

SHERIFF. Not really.

PRINCE. Joust?

SHERIFF. Not well.

PRINCE. Come now, certainly there must be something else you can do.

SHERIFF. Well, I don't mean to brag, but I have been known to make a mean loaf of bread. *directly in front of throne*

~~FAWNING LADIES *(big smiles).* BREAD!~~ *walk to UR stairs*

PRINCE. Oh. Well, that's very commendable, Sheriff. But at this point of the story I do think a bake-off might be a tad anti-climactic, don't you? *walk over to him*

SHERIFF. Wait! Yes! There is something at which I know I am the very, *very* best. In this sport, I am the incontestable champion! I have entered countless tournaments and have always won! Why, Your Majesty, I know Robin Hood could never compete with me! I am sure of it!

PRINCE. Wonderful! I knew you wouldn't let me down, Sheriff! Come! Tell me all about your secret talent as we make the necessary arrangements! *walk off UR*

(As the lights dim, the SHERIFF and PRINCE exit with the FAWNING LADIES following. The MERRY MEN, silhouetted, enter and change the scene to Sherwood Forest. TOWN'S GUY enters.)

TOWN'S GUY. Ah, plans, plots and intrigue. It seems that evil never rests. And so, good folk, we return again to Sherwood Forest. Just when Robin and the Merry Men thought things were finally going right, a shocking message had just been sent their way.

(The MERRY MEN are using LITTLE JOHN as a table. ALLAN has a Yahtzee dice roller. As lights come up he exclaims.)

ALLAN. YAHTZEE!

(ROBIN enters running.)

ROBIN. Another bull's-eye! That's my six-hundredth in a row! The Prince and the Sheriff will rue the day they came against Robin Hood of Sherwood Forest. I am unbeatable. *(Holds up his bow and strikes a heroic pose.)*
TOWN'S GUY. Robin, a shocking message has just been sent your way! *(Holds up message.)*
ROBIN. Not now, Town's Guy. I am posing. *(Smiles a heroic smile.)*
TOWN'S GUY. But this is really important.
ROBIN. Nothing could be more important than striking bull's-eye after bull's-eye!
TOWN'S GUY. Robin, they've changed the sport for the tournament.

ROBIN *(looks at TOWN'S GUY)*. What?!

TOWN'S GUY. Listen! *(Reads from paper.)* "His Royal Highness hereby decrees that the game for the tournament be changed. What was once to be an archery tournament, will now be a battle of bowling."

ROBIN *(drops bow and arrow and grabs the message)*. WHAT?!?! Give me that! *(Looks over the paper.)* BOWLING! This is the most ridiculous thing I've ever heard! We're in medieval England! You fence, or you joust! You don't bowl!

WILL. Well, boss, it looks like the times, they are a-changin'.

ROBIN. But I can't be seen bowling! I'm a great character of literature! Great characters of literature don't bowl!

ALLAN. Well, sir, maybe you can be the first. Then, other great characters of literature will follow in your footsteps.

ROBIN. Oh, right! Yes, I'm sure someday you'll open up a novel and find Madame Bovary picking up a seven-ten split at Flaubert's[*] Bowl-o-Rama! I DON'T THINK SO!

TUCK. My son, stay calm. Remember, good will always triumph over evil.

ROBIN. Friar, I don't think you understand. I can't be seen bowling because… *(Looks down at the floor.)* I don't know how to bowl.

MEN *(gasp, then, to AUDIENCE, in unison)*. OH, SHOCK AND DISBELIEF!

ROBIN. It looks as though I am going to fail the Lady Marian and the good people of England. I have fought so hard to help the poor and now I face defeat. True, I

---

[*] Pronounced: "flo-bear."

may be brave, trustworthy and kind...but alas, Merry Men, I am no bowler. *(Sits on the ground and puts his head into his hands.)*

TOWN'S GUY. Ah, Robin, things may not be as desperate as they seem.

ROBIN. Have you a suggestion, Town's Guy?

TOWN'S GUY. Better yet, I think I have a solution to the problem.

ROBIN. Then speak, I listen with both ears.

TOWN'S GUY. Well, the tournament was changed because the Sheriff and Prince discovered that you are the best archer in all the land, no doubt.

ROBIN. No doubt.

TOWN'S GUY. So they picked something that the Sheriff is the very best at, no doubt.

ROBIN. No doubt.

TOWN'S GUY. So they chose bowling because the Sheriff is the very best bowler in all the land, no doubt.

ROBIN *(getting aggravated)*. NO DOUBT! AND YOUR POINT IS...?

TOWN'S GUY. My point is, they missed one small detail in choosing a new sport for the tournament. The Sheriff of Nottingham may be a master bowler, but he is not the very best bowler in all the land... *(Pause.)* I am! *(They all turn and look at the TOWN'S GUY.)*

ROBIN. What? You?! The greatest bowler in all the land?

TOWN'S GUY. Yep!

ROBIN. But how?

TOWN'S GUY. Well, I was considered one of the lowly poor. I was never allowed to play on any of the royal leagues. The Sheriff and Prince have no idea that I am the finest bowler there is!

TUCK. This is wonderful news! Robin, the Town's Guy can enter the tournament. He'll win, give the gold to the poor, and Marian won't have to marry the Sheriff.

TOWN'S GUY. That's right! She'll marry me! *(ROBIN shoots a look of death to the TOWN'S GUY.)* It's a joke!

ROBIN. Swell. You'll win the tournament, save the poor, marry Marian and live happily ever after. Well, I guess I'm not the most important person in this play anymore. *(To TOWN'S GUY.)* You are! Congratulations! Well, I won't get in your way. Farewell to you all. *(Begins to exit.)*

WILL. Boss! You don't mean to tell us that you're quitting!

ALLAN. How can you quit now when we've come this far?

TUCK. The men are right, Robin! You can't abandon all of us who count on you.

ROBIN. For shame! For shame on me! You're right! I am not a quitter! I am Robin Hood, the most popular person in all the land! I shall not rest until England is safe once again. You should never give up the fight if you're fighting for what's right! *(Looks to AUDIENCE, points to them and says quickly.)* Did you all get that? Good. *(To TOWN'S GUY.)* Town's Guy, you must teach me how to bowl. Teach me now. That's an order.

TOWN'S GUY. No, Robin, I won't.

ROBIN. What do you mean, you won't? I said that's an order.

TOWN'S GUY. Robin, I'm your friend. You shouldn't order me around. If you want my help you can ask for it nicely. Because just because someone is popular, doesn't mean they can order their friends around and boss them all over the place. *(Looks to AUDIENCE, points to them and says quickly.)* Did you all get that? *(Directly into ROBIN's face.)* GOOD!

ROBIN *(after a pause)*. You're right. I have treated you badly. Town's Guy, will you please do me the honor of teaching me how to bowl? *(ROBIN extends his hand in friendship.)*

TOWN'S GUY. It will be my pleasure, Robin Hood of Sherwood. *(They shake hands.)*

MEN *(to AUDIENCE, in unison)*. HOORAY!

ROBIN. See, Merry Men? Even the most popular person in all the land must be humble at times. And as we all know, I possess thousands of praiseworthy qualities. But out of them all...HUMILITY IS ONE OF MY FINEST! *(MERRY MEN applaud ROBIN. He waves to them in acknowledgment.)* Yes, thank you! Huzzah, huzzah!

TOWN'S GUY *(to AUDIENCE)*. He hasn't grasped the point yet. But hey, it's a start.

ROBIN. Merry Men, I have a plan! I shall disguise myself and go to the tournament. Then, when I win, I shall claim Lady Marian's hand and declare the Prince a traitor! At that point, I will need your help. But until that moment, men, you are to *(stresses this point)* ...hide in the trees.

MEN *(in unison)*. Hide in the trees?

ROBIN. Yes, hide in the trees. *(Exit.)*

TOWN'S GUY. Robin, it's time to get to work. We only have one day to make you the greatest bowler in all the land.

ROBIN. Right you are, teacher! To work! *(Exit.)*

TOWN'S GUY. Robin Hood wasn't one to back down from a challenge! He was determined to conquer the sport of bowling before dawn. *(The sounds of bowling pins being knocked down are heard.)* As time passed, Robin listened carefully, memorized my every instruction. He never took a break in the grueling hours of practice. He embedded every rule of the game in his mind.

(Bowling sounds stop. ROBIN walks into the light and stands next to the TOWN'S GUY. The following exchange goes quickly.)

ROBIN. Town's Guy! I have mastered the game of bowling! I'm sure I know exactly what I'm talking about! I seize my rolling globe...
TOWN'S GUY. You take your bowling ball...
ROBIN. Point it midway...
TOWN'S GUY. Aim it center...
ROBIN. Spin it down the aisle...
TOWN'S GUY. Roll it down the lane...
ROBIN. And restrain it from the sewer.
TOWNS GUY. Stay out of the gutter.
ROBIN. Precisely! *(Calls to MERRY MEN offstage.)* Merry Men, it is official! I am an expert bowler.
MEN *(offstage in unison)*. HOORAY!
ROBIN. Now watch and marvel as I knock down all the bobby pins! *(Exits.)*
TOWN'S GUY *(yells after him)*. BOWLING PINS! *(To AUDIENCE.)* It's going to be a long night. Mr. Technical Director, if you please, make the hands of time spin quickly. Bring us to the castle and the day of the tournament.

(ROBIN enters.)

ROBIN. Town's Guy, look! I acquired an extra!
TOWN'S GUY. YOU PICKED UP A SPARE!

(They exit. Lights fade. Regal trumpet music plays as the MERRY MEN change the sets. The tournament set is hanging banners and flags on poles, etc. There should be some sort of "royal box" or a designated area with a chair or throne for the PRINCE to watch the tournament from. The TOWN'S GUY enters wearing a sports jacket over his tunic and tights. He has a microphone in his hand.)

TOWN'S GUY. Good morrow to you all, sports fans, and welcome to the first annual Bowling for the Hand of Lady Marian in Marriage Tournament. The crowd is the biggest we've ever seen here. And look! The royal family approaches!

(The PRINCE, MARIAN and LADY IN WAITING enter with the FAWNING LADIES following throwing rose petals.)

TOWN'S GUY. Why, here's the lovely Lady Marian… *(MARIAN waves as we hear cheers offstage. The LADY stands behind her.)* …and the ruler of our land…THE EVIL PRINCE JOHN. *(The PRINCE waves.)*
MEN *(offstage in unison)*. BOO, HISS! BOO, HISS!

Act II ROBIN HOOD 59

(PRINCE looks around in bewilderment. He sits. The SHERIFF enters and begins to prepare for the tournament.)

PRINCE *(to MARIAN)*. I don't see your beloved Robin Hood, my dear. Perhaps he realized he has been outsmarted.
MARIAN *(looking out in the crowd for ROBIN)*. Do not count him out yet, oh bunion breath.
PRINCE. If I were you, I'd start thinking of where I'd like to go on my honeymoon.
MARIAN. You know, the Sheriff may not be as good a bowler as you think! *(The SHERIFF rolls the bowling ball offstage. We hear the pins drop. The repeats should happen quickly in succession.)*
TOWN'S GUY. Strike for the Sheriff!
MARIAN *(to PRINCE)*. So he got lucky. *(The SHERIFF rolls the bowling ball offstage. We hear the pins drop.)*
TOWN'S GUY. Strike for the Sheriff!
MARIAN *(to PRINCE)*. Two strikes doesn't mean I should plan a honeymoon. *(The SHERIFF rolls the bowling ball offstage. We hear the pins drop.)*
TOWN'S GUY. Strike for the Sheriff!
MARIAN *(to PRINCE)*. You know, I've heard Cancun is lovely this time of year. Oh, I cannot bear to watch this. Call me when it's over. *(Begins to leave, then stops.)* May hangnails create anarchy amongst your fingers and your toes. *(Curtsies and exits.)*
TOWN'S GUY. What an unbelievable day is ahead of us. This Super Bowl of bowling is being held at none other than the royal castle itself! Why, just take a look at the

beautiful grounds and the lush landscape that surrounds us.

(The MERRY MEN enter disguised as trees. They are covered with bark and hold branches with leaves. LITTLE JOHN is crying softly.)

WILL. We look stupid!
ALLAN. Friar, are you sure this is what Robin meant when he said "hide in the trees"?
TUCK. Quiet, please! We must remain out of sight until Robin is ready to execute his plan.
WILL. Fine! But if I see any squirrels gathering nuts for the winter, I'm outta here.[*]
ALLAN *(to LITTLE JOHN, who is still crying softly)*. Why are you crying?
LITTLE. I'm a weeping willow. *(WILL smacks him in the head with his branch.)* Ow!

(ROBIN enters. He wears his trademark green hat, but has "disguised" himself by wearing the novelty plastic glasses, nose and mustache.)

ROBIN. Men, get in place! Remember, after I win the tournament, I'll confront the Prince and Sheriff. Your signal to come out of hiding will be when I declare them to be tyrants and thieves. Don't forget, the signal words are *tyrants* and *thieves*
MEN *(loudly in unison)*. TYRANTS AND THIEVES!
ROBIN. SHHH!

---
[*] No crotch grabbing or anything like that. Again, let good taste prevail. This line may be cut if found questionable.

MEN *(quietly in unison)*. Tyrants and thieves!

ROBIN. Good! *(Takes his bowling shoes. The SHERIFF stares at ROBIN. ROBIN, trying to avoid him, sits as far as he can from him. The SHERIFF, noticing this, walks up to him.)*

SHERIFF *(looking at ROBIN suspiciously)*. Good morrow to you, sir.

ROBIN *(trying not to look him in the eye)*. Good morrow.

SHERIFF. I don't believe I've ever seen you in our kingdom before.

ROBIN *(turns from SHERIFF)*. No, no, I'm not from around here. *(Sits down with shoes.)*

SHERIFF. Well, let me introduce myself. I am the Sheriff of Nottingham.

ROBIN *(with his head turned away from SHERIFF, shakes his hand quickly)*. Pleased to meet you.

SHERIFF. And your name?

ROBIN *(pauses)*. My name?

SHERIFF. Yes, your name. I assume you have one.

ROBIN. Yes. Of course I have one. And my name is... *(Looks into his shoe.)* Dr. Scholl.

SHERIFF. Ah, a physician! Well, best of luck to you, Doctor.

ROBIN. Yes, thank you. Same to you, sir. *(SHERIFF walks center. ROBIN realizes he doesn't have time to put on his shoes, hands them to one of the MERRY MEN dressed as a tree. Joins SHERIFF.)*

TOWN'S GUY. And now, let us wait in anticipation for the starting signal from the ruler of this land...THE EVIL PRINCE JOHN.

MEN *(quickly in unison)*. BOO, HISS! BOO, HISS!

PRINCE *(looks at the trees, then waves a little flag).* I declare the tournament to commence. *(ROBIN and the SHERIFF mime rolling imaginary bowling balls. We hear bowling sound effects.)*

TOWN'S GUY. And what a thrill-a-minute tournament it turned out to be! A thousand strikes were scored. However, soon the bowlers began to drop out one by one. The Sheriff of Nottingham and Dr. Scholl were the only two bowlers left in the game. They continued to bowl nonstop for six hours. And the way things were going, it looked like the Prince was going to have to declare the tournament a hopeless tie.

PRINCE. Stop the tournament! I think the competitors could use a small break. I declare a two-minute timeout. *(He waves to the SHERIFF to join him. ROBIN crosses to the MEN—two of them fan ROBIN with their branches.)* Sheriff, what are we going to do? If you don't win soon, I shall have to declare the tournament a hopeless tie.

SHERIFF. Sire, I don't know what to say! This Dr. Scholl is not a better bowler than me. But he is certainly just as good.

PRINCE *(laughs).* Yes, he may be equal to you as a bowler, but can he match you at archery?

SHERIFF. Archery? What do you mean?

PRINCE. You may not be able to beat Dr. Scholl with a bowling ball, but you certainly can beat him with a bow an arrow! Sheriff, watch in awe as I belch forth brilliance! *(Walks downstage to AUDIENCE.)* Good people of England, these two master bowlers have reached a stalemate! So I have come up with an ingenious solution to end the tournament. The Sheriff and Dr. Scholl will each have one shot at a target with a bow and arrow. The best shot will be proclaimed the winner! *(ROBIN looks at the TOWN'S GUY, who gives ROBIN an enthusiastic "thumbs-up.")* Good people of England, if you would like to see a one-shot, winner-take-all finish, let me know by a round of applause. *(ROBIN, the TOWN'S GUY and the MERRY MEN stand behind the PRINCE and the SHERIFF and prompt AUDIENCE to cheer by giving them the "thumbs-up," applauding, etc.)* Boy! They really like this idea! So be it! The people have chosen! *(The TOWN'S GUY exits to get the bow. PRINCE snaps his fingers, a FAWNING LADY brings him a target.)* Lady in Waiting *(she walks over to him)*, this is the target for the tie-breaking shot. *(Points to the "trees"—the MERRY MEN.)* Choose a tree!

MEN. NO! *(In unison, scattering in all directions, screaming).* AHHHHHH!! *(Exit. All remaining on stage watch in amazement as the landscape disappears.)*

PRINCE *(pause, then to SHERIFF)*. Remind me to have the gardener cut back on the Miracle-Gro.

(THE TOWN'S GUY comes on with their bows and arrows.)

LADY *(to PRINCE with target in hand)*. Excuse me, Sire, but what should I do with this?
PRINCE. Good question. *(Looks offstage.)* Ah! Lady, look… *(Points offstage.)* there's a tree that isn't fleeing for its life in terror. Place the target upon that one.
LADY. Yes, Your Most High-Upness. *(Curtsies and exits.)*
PRINCE. Now I decree that the tie-breaker commence! *(To FAWNING LADIES.)* Ladies!

(FAWNING LADIES grab pom-poms and run center stage.)

FAWNING LADY 1. GIMMIE AN S!
FAWNING LADIES. S!
FAWNING LADY 1. GIMMIE AN H!
FAWNING LADIES. H!
FAWNING LADY 1. GIMMIE AN E!
FAWNING LADIES. E!
FAWNING LADY 1. GIMMIE AN R!
FAWNING LADIES. R!
FAWNING LADY 1. GIMMIE A… *(Can't remember how to spell it, she thinks hard.)* M!
FAWNING LADIES. M!
FAWNING LADY 1. GIMMIE AN I!
FAWNING LADIES. I!
FAWNING LADY 1. GIMMIE AN F!
FAWNING LADIES. F!
FAWNING LADY 1. WHAT DOES THAT SPELL?
FAWNING LADIES. SHERMIF! *(They wave their pom-poms.)* YEAAAHHH!

(LADIES run back to places and sit.)

TOWN'S GUY *(carrying a quiver and bow. Bewildered)*. The first shot will be taken by…the Shermif of Nottingham. *(TOWN'S GUY hands the SHERIFF the bow. The SHERIFF takes an imaginary arrow from the quiver, places it in the bow, aims and fires it offstage.)* BULL'S-EYE!
PRINCE *(jumps out of his throne and yells at the top of his lungs)*. YOU DA MAN! *(Looks at everyone, composes himself, and sits. FAWNING LADIES applaud.)*

TOWN'S GUY. Shot number two will be taken by Dr. Scholl. *(ROBIN takes an arrow, places it in the bow, aims and fires it offstage.)* BULL'S-EYE! UNBELIEVABLE! DR. SCHOLL HAS SPLIT THE SHERIFF'S ARROW!

FAWNING LADIES *(in shock)*. AHHHHHH!

SHERIFF. WHAT! THIS CAN'T BE HAPPENING!

TOWN'S GUY. DR. SCHOLL WINS! *(TOWN'S GUY prompts AUDIENCE to cheer. ROBIN waves in triumph.)*

ROBIN *(to AUDIENCE as he revels in the cheers)*. Yes, thank you. Huzzah, huzzah!

TOWN'S GUY *(to the LADY who is sitting in a corner)*. Lady in Waiting! Alert Lady Marian that a winner has been declared!

LADY. Oh sure, it'll be my pleasure. *(As she crosses to exit.)* I'm sorry. Was I sitting down for five minutes? *(Exits.)*

TOWN'S GUY. Congratulations, Doctor! I name you champion of the tournament. First, allow me to reward your victory with one thousand gold pieces!

(TOWN'S GUY hands ROBIN a pouch which ROBIN holds up in victory. The LADY IN WAITING and MARIAN enter.)

TOWN'S GUY. And now, may I take the pleasure of awarding you the grand prize of the day…the hand of Lady Marian in marriage! *(Holds microphone to his mouth.)* Lady Marian, behold the winner of the tournament! *(Holds mike to her face for a reply.)*

MARIAN *(pushes mike away)*. I DON'T CARE! I SHALL NEVER MARRY HIM!

TOWN'S GUY *(holds mike to his mouth)*. He has defeated all competitors, and receives your hand in marriage!
MARIAN *(pushes mike away)*. I DON'T CARE! I SHALL NEVER MARRY HIM!
TOWN'S GUY *(holds mike to his mouth)*. Lady Marian, meet your future husband, Dr. Scholl.
MARIAN *(pushes mike away)*. I DON'T CARE! I SHALL NEVER... *(Grabs microphone to her mouth and smiles.)* He's a doctor?
TOWN'S GUY *(places MARIAN's hand into ROBIN's)*. Congratulations, to you both! *(Bows and exits.)*
ROBIN. Dear lady, I cannot deceive you any longer. There is something you must know.
MARIAN. What is it?
ROBIN. The truth is, I am not a real doctor.
MARIAN. You're a chiropractor?
ROBIN. No! I mean, my name is not Dr. Scholl.
MARIAN. It's not?
ROBIN. Not at all! My real name is *(whips off disguise from his face and proclaims)* ROBIN HOOD OF SHERWOOD FOREST!
PRINCE & SHERIFF. WHAT?!?!
MARIAN. Do my eyes deceive me? Robin Hood, the winner of my hand in marriage?!
ROBIN. Indeed, my lady. And now I have another promise to keep. A promise to free the people of England from the hands of two men who are...VILLAINOUS and DECEITFUL!
MEN *(offstage)*. NOW, ROBIN?
ROBIN *(looks offstage)*. No, not yet. *(To PRINCE and SHERIFF.)* The poor will have a voice again. I'll liberate them from captors that are...CORRUPT and SINISTER!

MEN *(offstage)*. NOW, ROBIN?

ROBIN *(yells offstage)*. NO! NOT YET!

PRINCE *(to ROBIN)*. Villainous? Sinister? Such strong words you use, outlaw! Please note that the Sheriff and I would rather be referred to as "morally challenged."

SHERIFF. I agree. That has a more polite ring to it.

ROBIN. Morally challenged? Ha! How you find ways to hide the truth! The plain fact of the matter is, you Prince John and you Sheriff of Nottingham are nothing more than… *(Center, points to PRINCE and SHERIFF and as big as he can make it.)* TYRANTS AND THIEVES! *(Expecting the MERRY MEN to enter, but they don't. ROBIN pauses a moment and looks offstage. Then, in a louder voice shouts offstage.)* I SAID, the Prince and Sheriff are nothing more than TYRANTS AND THIEVES! *(Nothing. Annoyed.)* What? Doesn't anyone work for minimum wage anymore? *(Shouts to MEN offstage.)* NOW!!

(MERRY MEN enter, minus their tree garb, screaming all the way.)

MEN. AHHHHHH!! *(They "draw" their spoons from the sheaths.)* AH HA!

ROBIN. BEHOLD OUR MIGHT, EVIL-DOERS! WATCH AS WE BATTLE YOU TO DEFEAT!

PRINCE. Battle us? *(Laughs to SHERIFF.)* They're going to battle us. Oh that's good…that's very good. Robin Hood, if you think you, your five Merry Men and their oh-so-dangerous spoons…

SHERIFF. Ohhhhh! Save me from the spoons!

PRINCE. ...can overpower my military forces of twelve thousand, well, what can I say but, be my guest! *(The MERRY MEN look concerned.)*
ALLAN *(to PRINCE)*. Excuse me, did you say twelve thousand?
SHERIFF. Yes. And that's without the navy.
WILL. You know, as spokesman for the Merry Man Union, Local Chapter 9-0-8, may I say I'm really glad you brought that up.
ROBIN. Please, men! If freedom for England means we fight to the death, then we fight to the death!
PRINCE. If it's death you want, Robin Hood, it's death you shall have! I don't care who has won what! I AM RULER HERE! I WILL BECOME KING! I decree that Marian will marry the Sheriff today! But before she does, we will have a beheading!
SHERIFF. Your Highness, why don't we have *(gestures to include the MERRY MEN)* six beheadings! *(To MERRY MEN.)* We wouldn't want anyone to feel left out!
PRINCE. Excellent idea, Sheriff! Call the guards and the executioners! *(Points to ROBIN and the MEN.)* CUT OFF THEIR HEADS!
LITTLE *(just catching on)*. CUT OFF OUR HEADS! THAT COULD BE FATAL!
WILL *(to ROBIN)*. Ya know, if I get beheaded, I want a raise.
ROBIN. Knock it off! Where is your spirit, men? We must stand here and fight for what is right! *(Behind ROBIN's back the MERRY MEN are trying to "Shhhh" him and ALLAN is mouthing to the PRINCE that ROBIN is "only kidding.")* Prince, bring forth your armies! Pummel us

with your weapons! Our blood, indeed, may be spilt! But we are devoted to our cause!
PRINCE. So be it!
SHERIFF *(as he looks offstage)*. Your Highness, the guards approach!
PRINCE *(shouts offstage)*. GUARDS OF THE ROYAL ARMY, I COMMAND YOU TO ATTACK!
ROBIN. ALL RIGHT, MEN! SCATTER!

(Lights dim. There should be silhouetted bedlam onstage. CAST MEMBERS running and screaming everywhere. This should last six to ten seconds, no longer. Then, heard over all the screaming...)

TOWN'S GUY. JUST ONE MOMENT!! *(Lights up to reveal the TOWN'S GUY center stage, quite out of breath.)* THERE WILL BE NO BATTLE TODAY!
PRINCE. Peasant! What do you think you're doing?! How dare you interrupt the battle!

(LITTLE JOHN, still scattering, runs onstage, screaming with his arms flailing.)

LITTLE. AHHHHHH!!
ROBIN *(to LITTLE JOHN)*. STOP IT!!
TOWN'S GUY *(shouts offstage to the "army")*. Hold your attack, soldiers! *(To EVERYONE.)* I have just come from the royal campgrounds. *(Holds up a rolled-up scroll.)* I hold in my hand...A MESSAGE FROM THE KING! *(ALLAN pulls out a kazoo and plays a few regal notes in a fanfare.)*

PRINCE. LIAR! Liar, liar, tights on fire! This cannot be! King Richard is hundreds of miles away! You were just standing here no more than two minutes ago. How could you possibly have a message from the King?

TOWN'S GUY. Tell me, Highness, have you ever hear of fade out and segue to next scene?

PRINCE. No!

TOWN'S GUY. It's this wonderful effect that can be achieved with the help of our friend, Mr. Technical Director. *(TOWN'S GUY, ROBIN, MARIAN, MERRY MEN and LADY IN WAITING all wave into the audience to the technical director.)*

SHERIFF. They're all mad, Sire!

TOWN'S GUY. Not at all! Mr. Technical Director can fade out a person of his choice and put them in a totally different place.

MARIAN *(to PRINCE)*. It's true! I've tried it on occasion. It's really quite a hoot!

TOWN'S GUY. I asked him to take me to the royal campgrounds. There, I found King Richard and explained to him the critical situation. He quickly gave me this decree to bring back to you, Robin Hood. *(TOWN'S GUY hands ROBIN the document.)*

ROBIN. Thank you, Town's Guy. *(To AUDIENCE.)* At long last, good people of England, hear the words of your king… *(Again, ALLAN pulls out a kazoo and plays a few regal notes in a fanfare as ROBIN unrolls the decree and begins to read.)* "I, King Richard, King of all England, command the following proclamation come to pass. First, I decree that the tax money, which was stolen by my brother, John and the Sheriff of Nottingham, be rightfully returned to the people of England."

MEN. HOORAY!

ROBIN. "I next decree that the hand of my dear niece, the Lady Marian, be given in marriage to Robin Hood of Sherwood Forest." *(ROBIN blows MARIAN a kiss.)*

MEN. HOORAY!

ROBIN. "As reward for their bravery, I enlist the Merry Men into the King's royal guards, thus boosting their salaries substantially above minimum wage."

MEN. HOORAY!

ROBIN. "I proclaim that our lady-in-waiting be named as the Kingdom's Emergency Broadcast System, because every time she screams, I can hear it here in Istanbul."

MEN. HOORAY! *(LADY quickly runs center with a big smile and winds up to scream.)*

EVERYONE. NO! *(LADY curtsies and stands next to MERRY MEN.)*

ROBIN *(with great enthusiasm)*. "In honor of the Town's Guy and his monumental loyalty to the throne... *(TOWN'S GUY takes center with a big smile.)* I declare that... *(Less enthusiasm.)* bowling become the national sport of England."

MEN *(less enthusiastic)*. Hooray. *(TOWN'S GUY shrugs and stands by men.)*

ROBIN. "In regard to the Sheriff of Nottingham..."

MEN *(to the SHERIFF in unison)*. Uh-oh...

PRINCE *(to SHERIFF)*. Well, you're on your own.

ROBIN. "I terminate him from the position of sheriff effective immediately. Then, I banish him from England forever!"

MEN. HOORAY!

ROBIN. "And, as for my jealous and conniving brother, THE EVIL PRINCE JOHN..."

MEN *(in unison to AUDIENCE)*. BOO, HISS! BOO, HISS!

ROBIN. "I declare him officially disowned from the royal family! From this day forward, his title will be only that of: John, the character formally known as Prince."

MEN. HOORAY!

ROBIN. "I now join my royal army en route back home to England. But until my arrival, I declare that Robin Hood of Sherwood rule in my absence. I place my beloved country in his trusted hands."

MEN. HOORAY!

PRINCE *(grabs decree from ROBIN)*. Give me that! I don't believe a word of this!

SHERIFF. Nor do I! This is just a scheme to make us surrender our power!

PRINCE. The Sheriff is right! Do you actually expect us to believe that some mystery person, hidden in the dark, can transport us to another place. And he does this by flashing magic lights?! This is all a trick to fool us! Well, it's not going to work! There is nothing you can do that will make us believe this wild tale! Do you understand me? Nothing, I say!

ROBIN. Oh, really? *(ROBIN looks at the TOWN'S GUY who smiles and gives ROBIN a "thumbs-up.")* Mr. Technical Director, if you please! All right everyone, TAKE COVER!

(The lights flicker, spooky music plays. The FAWNING LADIES scream. ROBIN runs to MARIAN and the LADY IN WAITING. The MERRY MEN run to the FAWNING LADIES. Each of the MERRY MEN puts his arm around a FAWNING LADY to protect her. The SHERIFF and PRINCE divide and separate to R and L. The easiest

Act II ROBIN HOOD 73

way for them to fade out is for them to wave their arms in circles and exit, one L, one R, quickly running backward. You want the impression they're being sucked offstage. This is a good spot for special effects such as a strobe light, flash pads or a blast of smoke or fog. It's not necessary, but it's nice.)

PRINCE *(panicking)*. Ah! What's happening!
SHERIFF. Highness, I feel funny!
PRINCE & SHERIFF. WHOOOOAAAA!! AHHHHHH!! *(They exit.)*

(Lights up. Each MERRY MAN gazes at his FAWNING LADY with his mouth open. The FAWNING LADIES gaze back. They're frozen, staring at each other, completely oblivious to any other action onstage. ROBIN runs center and proclaims:)

ROBIN. LET IT BE KNOWN THAT ENGLAND IS SAFE ONCE AGAIN! *(To the TOWN'S GUY.)* Where did he send them?
TOWN'S GUY. I'm not sure. He said something about fading them into a bad community theatre production of *Cats*. I have no idea what that means *(points out into the dark)*, but he thought it was hysterical. *(TOWN'S GUY and ROBIN wave to the technical director.)*
ROBIN. May I have your attention, Merry Men. *(Looks at MEN, no response. The MEN stand frozen, still gazing at their FAWNING LADY.)* Merry Men... *(No response. MERRY MEN still frozen, still gazing.)* Yodels.
MEN *(turn in unison and look at ROBIN)*. Huh?

ROBIN. The first thing I would like to do as temporary ruler of this country is…

LITTLE. Wait! Let me guess, erect a statue of yourself to honor your popularity?

ROBIN. No.

ALLAN. Write your good deeds in all the history books?

ROBIN. No.

WILL. Fly flags with your picture on them because you're the most important person in this play?

ROBIN. No, but that's good! The first thing I would like to do is…thank you, Merry Men…and you too, Town's Guy… *(Waves out in the dark.)* and of course, Mr. Technical Director, as well. I would not have been able to save England without your help. I am most fortunate to have you as friends.

TOWN'S GUY & MEN. WOW!

MARIAN. Oh, Robin, that was lovely.

ROBIN. Yes, Marian, that was humility. It's one of my finest qualities, you know!

MARIAN. Bravo, my love!

ROBIN. Yes, thank you. *(Waves in triumph to her.)* Huzzah, huzzah!

TUCK. My son, it's time to follow one of the King's commands and have a wedding!

ALL *(to AUDIENCE in unison)*. A wedding! Oh, happy day! *(Everyone runs center to join ROBIN and MARIAN. Each MERRY MAN has his arm around his FAWNING LADY.)*

ROBIN. Oh happy day, indeed! *(To MEN.)* Would you like to stand up for me as my best men, oh Merry Men of Sherwood?

MEN. SURE WOULD!

MARIAN. Good Lady in Waiting, will you do me the pleasure of being my maiden of honor?

LADY. Oh, I would love to. But let's get one thing straight. I am *not* wearing one of those sea-foam green things with some sort of gladiola growing out of my shoulder, so you can get that idea our of your head right now.

MARIAN *(with an uneasy smile to ROBIN)*. She said yes.

ROBIN. Good. *(All gather center. Lights flicker and begin to dim. Appropriate upbeat "happy ending" music should play. ROBIN looks out and speaks to AUDIENCE.)* The good people of England will once again flourish in health and prosperity. This experience has taught us all a few good lessons of life...*especially me.* And now, with great pleasure, I say, Mr. Technical Director, take us all to the church! Farewell to you all, gentle folk of England! May you know nothing but happiness from this day forward! *(He puts his arm around MARIAN. To MERRY MEN.)* Ready men...SCATTER!

MEN. AHHHHHH!!

(The MERRY MEN, along with the TOWN'S GUY, LADY IN WAITING and the FAWNING LADIES, scatter, screaming and waving their arms. They exit in all directions and get offstage quickly. Just as everyone is offstage, ROBIN and MARIAN, center, kiss. As their lips meet, LITTLE JOHN, not done scattering, runs across stage behind them, screaming with his arms flailing.)

LITTLE. AHHHHHH!! *(Exits. As soon as LITTLE JOHN is offstage...blackout.)*

CURTAIN—END OF PLAY

PRODUCTION NOTES

CASTING: To expand the cast size, an additional scene can be added after Robin meets the Sheriff and Marian for the first time in Act One. This will increase the speaking roles and bring the cast from 14 to 20. The characters in the new scene can be male or female.

Gender changes:

BEULAH or BYRON
LADY or LORD LAUGHALOT
MARY or MARTY

LIONEL or LENORE
DONALD or DONNA
DEBBIE or DENNIS

The following is the point of the script where the new scene is to be inserted. This is found on page 19.

TOWN'S GUY. When he learned of Marian's allegiance to Robin Hood, he was swift to engage her to the Sheriff of Nottingham, thus securing his position. This now takes us out of the flashback and back to the present time. And so, friends, it seems I'm finished here. I am going back to town. *(To ROBIN.)* WHERE I'M APPRECIATED! *(To AUDIENCE.)* I hope we'll see each other again. Farewell. *(Bows and exits.)*

[Begin additional scene:

ROBIN. Friar! Have the applicants for the Merry Men positions arrived yet?
TUCK. Yes, my son, they have.

ROBIN. Good! Bring them forth, be they men or be they women. After all, we here in Sherwood Forest are an equal opportunity employer and do not discriminate. *(FRIAR leaves to get applicants.)* Merry Men, I have placed a help wanted ad in the Sherwood Forest Daily Gazette. We will add to our merry band. Remember, number one: there is strength in numbers, and number two: the more the merrier. *(Cracks himself up while the MERRY MEN look at him with no expression.)* Get it? *(No response.)* You're *Merry* Men. *(No response.)* Ooh, tough crowd.

(FRIAR enters with the applicants. LITTLE JOHN runs over to ROBIN, gets on all fours and is used as "a table" throughout the interviews.)

FRIAR. Beulah of Bellowsbank
ROBIN. So, Ms. Bellowsbank, what prior experience have you had at being merry?
BEULAH/BRYON. Well sir, I was merry at Christmas.
ROBIN. I see. Have you had other occasions at which to be merry?
BEULAH. Well, I've been jovial at times, sir. That's just like being merry only louder.
ROBIN. Fine. You're hired. Pick up your spoon and report to work.
BEULAH. Yes, sir!
ROBIN. Next.
MARY. Hello sir, I'm Mary.
ROBIN. Ah, I see. So Mary, are you merry?

MARY. Yes sir, I'm most merry. In college I majored in merry, minored in merriment and got my master's in merrymaking.
ROBIN. Oh, what college?
MARY. Marymount.
ROBIN. Marvelous. Get a spoon.
MARY. Thank you.
ROBIN. Next.
LADY LAUGHALOT. Hello, sir, I'm Lady Laughalot.
ROBIN. So, Lady Laughalot, what experience have you had at being merry?
LADY LAUGHALOT. Very extensive experience, sir. For the past five years I've written the opening monologue for David Lettermerryman.
ROBIN. You're hired, get a spoon. *(To FRIAR.)* I love that show! Next!
LIONEL. I'm sorry, sir, I think I'm at the wrong interview. I thought I was applying for a Jolly Good Fellow.
ROBIN. Oh. Well, are you a Jolly Good Fellow?
LIONEL. That nobody can deny.
ROBIN. Close enough. *(Hands him a spoon.)*
LIONEL. Thank you, sir.
ROBIN. Next! *(A very stiff-looking guy walks up to ROBIN.)* Hello. Who might you be?
DONALD *(a very expressionless, monotone voice)*. Donald.
ROBIN. So, Donald, are you merry?
DONALD *(almost robotic)*. Yes.
ROBIN. Are you sure?
DONALD. Yes, I'm merry.
ROBIN. Well then…why don't you give me your most merriest expression?
DONALD *(pauses, then without expression)*. Yowza.

ROBIN. Well, I guess that'll do. Grab a spoon.
DONALD. What about my sister?
ROBIN. Your sister?
DONALD. Yeah. Debbie.
DEBBIE *(steps forward, as stiff and expressionless as DONALD; waves to ROBIN, and in a monotone)*. Yowza.
ROBIN. Okay, fine. But you have to share a spoon.

(DONALD and DEBBIE get a spoon and join the other MERRY MEN.)

End of additional scene. Continue as written, with:]

ROBIN. Oh, Friar, what to do, what to do.
FRIAR. My son, why don't I go to town to see if there is news. Perhaps an answer to our problem lies there. *(Etc.)*

———

You may add some or all of the new characters, just adapt their genders appropriately throughout the rest of the text. However, if you do use the new scene, it is best to bring at least three new characters to make the scene worthwhile. Please note: Any new female Merry Men will still be referred to as Merry Men. If you want to cast all the new Merry Men with men, just cut the lines: "Bring them forth, be they men or be they women. After all, we here in Sherwood Forest are an equal opportunity employer and do not discriminate" from the new scene. You can also cast the Town's Guy as the Town's Girl—again, adapting the character's gender throughout the show. The new Merry Men speak all of the men's collective lines such as, "BOO, HISS! BOO, HISS!" and "SURE WOULD!" etc. To add even more characters, cast the Guards, the Rich Man and the Poor Lady singly. You can also add extra Merry Men. This will bring the cast to 25 or more.

To condense the cast size: If you require a smaller cast, simply cut the Fawning Ladies, their lines and all references to them. You'll have to change the Town's Guy/Girl's line in the tournament to: "The first shot will be taken by the Sheriff of Nottingham," instead of: "The first shot will be taken by...the Sher*mif* of Nottingham." Make sure you double the Guards, Rich Man and Poor Lady. This reduces the cast from 14 to 10.

SETS: Sets can be as simple or elaborate as you like. One suggestion for sets is sturdy, two-sided turning flats—trees on one side, stone walls on the other. (A triangular set piece on wheels, may also be used instead of a two-sided flat to give you more variety of scenes.) As it states in the stage directions, the Merry Men turn them to form the forest or the castle. Another suggestion for sets is to have a curtain with trees or a forest scene painted on it that can open in the center or be pulled completely offstage right or left. The castle scene is behind the curtain. This way, you simply close the curtain to go back to Sherwood Forest. When changing scenes, it is very important not to stop the play's action. The changes should be done during the specified stage directions in the script and flow smoothly throughout the show. Not doing this properly will cause the production to become disjointed. I've directed productions using both types of set pieces. I preferred the Sherwood Forest curtain to the two-sided flats, but both types of sets worked well.

COSTUMES: Costumes for the characters should follow a general storybook look but lean toward cartoon rather than romantic, if possible.

ROBIN HOOD should be the best-dressed of all the men of the forest. Earth tones with perhaps a hunter green cape that falls just below his tunic. He should have boots and wear his trademark Robin Hood cap complete with feather. (Should you not know what this looks like, rent the Robin Hood movie with Errol Flynn.)

THE MERRY MEN (even if they are girls) should wear tunics with long sleeve T-shirts, big leather belts, and tights. An alternative to tights (for those actors too macho to wear them) are dyed long-john bottoms. It's also convenient for the tunics to have pockets so the Merry Men can easily carry their small props, such as the cards, kazoo, a place to put their yodels, etc. Their footwear should be boots, such as lace-up work boots (no obvious cowboy boots). If boots are not available or affordable, the Merry Men can wear old-fashioned, Converse high-top basketball sneakers. They *do not* wear high-tech Nike stuff. Friar Tuck's costume is a typical brown, floor-length robe with a robe belt. A burlap fabric does well for this costume. A friar is not a priest, do not confuse the two. Please make sure the Merry Men and Robin have *large, wooden* mixing spoons.

PRINCE JOHN should have a crown, of course. He wears a tunic and can also wear a turtleneck under his tunic for a different look, and tights. His cape should be floor-length. His footwear: slip-on leather house slippers. A jeweled medallion around his neck is a nice touch, as well as lots of big jeweled rings on his fingers. However, try to avoid making him look like Liberace.

THE SHERIFF OF NOTTINGHAM should be costumed in a tunic—your basic dark, bad-guy colors, and tights or dyed long-johns. His cape should be shorter than Prince John's cape. Medieval-looking, black leather gloves are a nice touch for him. He wears dark leather slippers or boots.

LADY MARIAN, THE LADY IN WAITING and the FAWNING LADIES wear floor-length gowns, preferably with empire waists. The colors of the Lady in Waiting's and Fawning Ladies' gowns should be muted in comparison to Marian's gown. The Fawning Ladies' dresses can be identical or match either in color and/or style, if possible. Lady Marian should have the prettiest dress. Please don't make the girls look like they are going to the prom or walking down the aisle in cousin Ursula's wedding. Some theatre companies think the audience won't notice, but they always do. Then everyone goes out after the show and talks about it over coffee. Trust me, I've done it—so have you, you know you have.

Something fun you might want to consider—Robin and the Sheriff can wear large bowling shirts for the tournament. These shirts should be large enough to fit nicely over their tunics. A fun touch is to put the name of a local business on the back of their shirts. (Especially if the local business is willing to sponsor your production.) If you do not wish to use a local business, the Sheriff's shirt should say: THE JOUST JOINT, and Robin's shirt should say: WOODHAVEN LUMBER. Make the logos readable to the audience, otherwise it becomes a distraction. It is not mandatory that these characters have bowling shirts. If they do, however, they should take off the shirts during the Prince's "tie-breaking" monologue to the audience. They should be out of the shirts before they take their tie-breaking shots.

PROP LIST

Act I

Sherwood Forest – Scene 1
    Merry Men: playing cards
    Allan: pewter mug and coaster (mug should hook onto Allan's belt after it's used)

Another part of the forest – Scene 2
    Rich Man: bag of money
    Poor Lady: baby wrapped in a blanket
    Sheriff: pouch of gold
    Marian: small wooden chest and large jeweled ring for her finger
    Merry Men: large, wooden mixing spoons with "sword"-type handles which they keep with them throughout the rest of the show, preferably in a sheath or tucked into their belts

Sherwood Forest – Scene 3
    Allan: Slinky

Throne Room – Scene 4
    Fawning Ladies: 4 baskets with rose petals
    Fawning Lady 1: nail file
    Fawning Lady 2: fan

Sherwood Forest – Scene 5
    Friar: large box of Yodels (a brand of cake), proclamation
    Robin: target
    Allan: bow and quiver

Marian's Chamber – Scene 6
    Dress dummy with wedding dress
    Lady: wedding veil, arrow with message

Sheriff: dagger
Robin: spoon
Town's Guy: bouquet of roses
Fawning Ladies: rose petals

Sherwood Forest – Scene 7
Merry Men: earrings

Act II

Throne Room – Scene 2
Sheriff: clipboard with paper
Fawning Lady 1: nail polish
Fawning Lady 2: magazine (Glamour, Cosmo, Seventeen, or whatever you want)
Fawning Lady 3: eyebrow tweezers and small mirror or compact
Fawning Ladies: white accordion-folded wedding bells, "Just Married" sign

Sherwood Forest – Scene 3
Allan: Yatzee dice roller
Robin: bow and quiver
Town's Guy: message

Tournament – Scene 4
Town's Guy: microphone, bow and quiver, pouch of gold, proclamation
Merry Men: tree branches and tree trunks
Robin: plastic "Groucho Marx" nose, glasses and mustache, bowling shoes
Fawning Lady 1: target—a square piece of cloth, approximately 24 in., with a red target on it that can be easily folded and carried on by the Lady without hassle
Fawning Ladies: pompoms
Allan: kazoo

SOME ADDITIONAL CHARACTER DESCRIPTIONS

ROBIN HOOD: He's quite impressed with himself. (A cross between Dudley DoRight and *Frasier's* Niles Crane.) To feed his ego, one must fill a void the size of the Grand Canyon. However, his heart is good, for his mission is to help the homeless and poor of England.

LADY MARIAN: She is the niece of King Richard and Prince John. She is also Robin's true love. She is a cross between Emma Thompson and Miss Piggy. She is kind, charming and shares Robin's quest to aid the needy. However, she has a strange obsession with skin conditions.

PRINCE JOHN: He's typically evil, selfish, greedy and has positively no regard for the welfare of England or its people. Should be largely despicable.

SHERIFF OF NOTTINGHAM: Shares all of Prince's prime qualities. Moreover, he is a master sportsman and Robin's chief rival. He also hopes to marry Marian.

TOWN'S GUY: Befriends Robin and helps him out of a few tight situations while teaching him some valuable lessons at the same time. Serves as the story's narrator.

LADY IN WAITING: Fed up with life in the castle.

THE MERRY MEN: Collectively, the Merry Men should behave somewhat like a pack of happy, but none-too-bright stray dogs.

DIRECTOR'S NOTES

DIRECTOR'S NOTES

DIRECTOR'S NOTES